Mama Penee
Transcending the Genocide

Uazuvara Ewald Kapombo Katjivena

University of Namibia Press
www.unam.edu.na/unam-press
unampress@unam.na
Private Bag 13301
Windhoek
Namibia

© Uazuvara Ewald Kapombo Katjivena, 2020

All rights reserved. No part of this publication may be reproduced, stored in any retrieval system or transmitted in any form, or by any means, e.g. electronic, mechanical, photocopying, recording or otherwise without prior written permission of the publisher.

Cover design and layout: Handmade Communications
Printed by: CTP Printers, Cape Town
Illustrations: Morteza Amari

ISBN   978-99916-42-51-2

The views and opinions expressed herein are the author's own and do not necessarily represent those of the University of Namibia.

Distribution
In Namibia by Namibia Book Market: www.namibiabooks.com
Internationally by the African Books Collective: www.africanbookscollective.com

Contents

Foreword – A Living Witness to History	v
Preface and Acknowledgements	xiii
Part One: Born to Survive	1
1. The Tree of Origins	3
2. Inherited Peace and the Threat of War	9
3. When Fear isn't Enough	15
4. The Long Journey	19
5. The Way to Survival	23
6. Pleasantness	27
7. Humiliation at Work	31
8. Mama Penee gets Married	37
9. Settling in Okakarara	41
Part Two: Challenging Power	47
1. When the Beat Changes, so Does the Dance	49
2. "What Did You Learn at School Today?"	53
3. Snakes and White Cattle	57
4. The Power of Interpretation	61
5. The Need to Know and Understand	65
6. Who is Hurt?	69
7. The Fable about the Stomach	73
8. Patches	75
9. Who Owns the Fruit?	77
10. The Languages God Speaks	81
11. Laundry	83
12. The Taste of Sugar	85
13. Childhood Friends Come Face to Face	89
14. Deplorable Acts	93
15. What is Freedom?	99
16. Accepting the End of Life	105
Bibliography	107
Who is Katjivena?	111

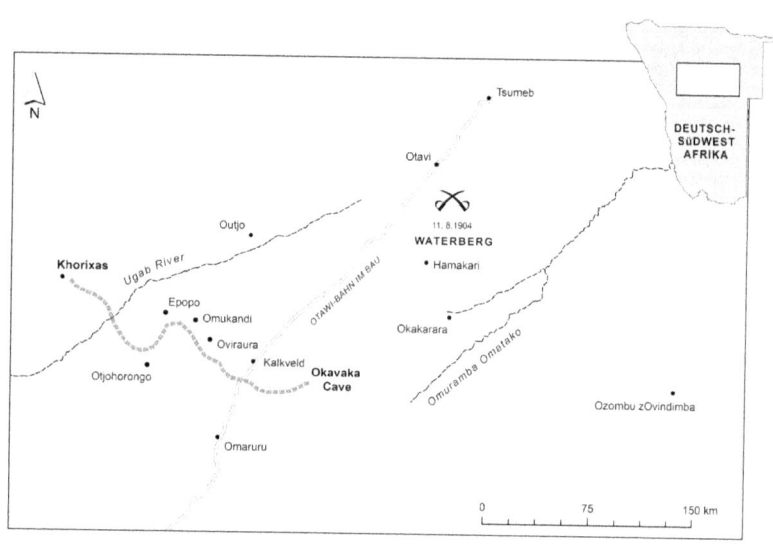

Map showing Jahohora's journey on foot from what they called the Okavaka Mountains to Khorixas in 1904.

Foreword

A Living Witness to History

In the 1950s, Mama Penee's grandsons had to learn by heart the history of Europe and the blessings of colonialism. It was generally assumed that the people of Africa had none of their own, and that before the arrival of colonialism and Christianity they lived as savages. Some people had a basis for this theory in racism. Others excused themselves by explaining that it was impossible to know anything about the indigenous society, as there was nothing written down.

In this book, however, we are given a clear picture of a historical consciousness which has been passed down through generations of Ovaherero by word of mouth. Where historical timelines have not existed, we meet legends and folk tales that explain how the world was created and how the Ovaherero came to be. All the different cultures in the world, including Christianity have their own Creation myths, which try to explain the most fundamental questions mankind has always had. The Ovaherero and those who live in current-day Namibia have their own versions.

Through a gentle portrait of Mama Penee, we are invited to experience a culture and religion based upon respect for mankind and the nature surrounding us, an awe of life, and the necessity of peace. It should make us reflect when we continually hear that Western cultural values are the best. Mama Penee has something to teach us.

It is the African storytelling tradition which we meet on paper in this unique book. A tradition which weaves together people's lives (and deaths) with the history of European imperialism, genocide, and the transition to a society governed by the South African rules of apartheid. The story contains many historical aspects, with people as active participants. Both German colonialism and the South African apartheid regime were human creations, and it was the Namibian people's indomitable strength and fighting spirit that consigned both these systems of domination to the scrap-heap of history.

Namibian history and the history of the family in this book deals with unimaginable evil, but also unimaginable good. Those who think that the past is dead and that it has nothing to do with the society we live in today should, through reading this book, come to realise that they are completely wrong.

Fortunately, many historians, including those with a Namibian background, have begun to give us a more comprehensive and realistic picture of the country's past. European sources can be interpreted differently and, not least, a new generation of German historians has shown how a new approach should be used. History isn't as it was. Instead, it has become more unpredictable. There are still many untold stories from Namibians in all parts of the country, and there has been far too little consideration taken of accounts from their side. This could also be of benefit to the historians who are tempted to focus on the heroes of the armed struggle in the north of the country from the 1960s on.

One of the main threads in Mama Penee's story is that of her youth under German colonialism. Germany was a foreign power that was mostly interested in seizing the cattle, grazing lands and valuable water-holes of the indigenous inhabitants. The Ovaherero themselves were put to work on the invader's property or, as in the case of Mama Penee, as a subservient and unwilling housemaid to her masters. This was an attack on both the livelihood of the Ovaherero and their culture. After increasing occupation of land and the arrival of even more German settlers, long periods of drought and cattle disease, there was no alternative for the Ovaherero than to launch a desperate attempt to throw off the yoke of foreign domination.

Uprisings against colonialism were happening all over Africa, but that was not enough for Kaiser Wilhelm II's military forces. At some time during the conflict, the idea of a "final solution" came into being. It was decreed that all Ovaherero, and after a while all the Nama as well, should be exterminated, their lands confiscated and given to the German soldiers and civilians who wanted to establish themselves in the country. The result of this has become known as "the first genocide of the 20th Century". When the UN established the Genocide Convention in 1948, their criteria for genocide matched exactly what had happened in Namibia forty years earlier. As research into genocide becomes more characterised by a global perspective, more and more examples from Africa are coming to light.

Mama Penee was a living witness to history, and her account is extremely important because so little has been done to document the atrocities committed by the Europeans. The contrast between the work done to uncover crimes and genocide committed on the European continent under the First and Second World Wars could not be greater.

Mama Penee's parents were amongst the first victims of the genocide in Namibia. She was only eleven years old in 1904 when she was witness to two peaceful, unarmed people being executed in cold blood before her eyes. Four years later, approximately 80% of the Ovaherero were dead, in addition to 50% of the Nama who were killed further south in the country. Many were shot, whilst others died of starvation and thirst in the desert (thus saving the Germans' ammunition).

Those who survived the fighting and the flight through the desert were captured and sent to concentration camps, where sickness and death awaited them. For the first time in history, the expression *konzentrationslager* entered the German vocabulary. There were death camps, work camps and camps where the Germans kept their sex slaves. The connections to the future and Hitler's Germany are many and frightening. We encounter them in the experimentation upon captives, in the race laws, in ethnically based extermination of *"Untermenschen"*, and the belief that the Germans were superior and had God on their side.

Many historians and social science researchers perceive the two World Wars, the Holocaust and the brutality of the Eastern Front as an inexplicable deviation in the behaviour of an otherwise great Western civilization. This book makes us realise that colonialism, racism, repression and genocide against the African people is actually the norm in European history. It was not just the dream of an ideological, racially pure Christian society which explains what happened in German South West Africa, just as on the Eastern Front during the Second World War we can identify the main drivers as land occupancy, control over natural resources, and areas for German settlement.

There was no peace, rebuilding, or compensation after the genocide. (The people of Namibia are still waiting for compensation. In 2015 Germany finally agreed to begin negotiations about this but the matter had still not been resolved by mid-2019). No one was repatriated to their land. Instead it was forbidden for the Ovaherero to own property or to live together in communities. They were also forced to wear a tin pendant around their necks marked with an H for Herero. The repression created tension in both the colonial system and the relationships between people, as evidenced by the account Mama Penee gives of her time spent with the German family who ruled her life, and the land once owned by her people.

Genocide and German colonialism shaped Mama Penee's life and the stories that she passed down through her family. She lived in a society which was built on military occupation, racism, expropriation of land and cultural repression. Germany's colonies were confiscated after the First World War which started as a European "tribal conflict", but also claimed many lives in Africa. On paper, it was Great Britain that governed Namibia after 1919, but it outsourced control to the neighbouring country of South Africa, which was in the process of establishing a socio-economic system that greatly resembled that of Namibia under German occupation. After the Second World War, this system was continued even though South Africa was asked to explain itself to the UN.

In the 1950s and 1960s, many of the former African colonies achieved independence, as evidenced in this book by the admiration expressed for Ghana and President Kwame Nkrumah. The new heads of state in Africa were not just concerned with their own liberty, but gave their support to the movements for freedom in other countries such as Namibia, Zimbabwe, Mozambique and Angola. They reached a significant victory in the UN in 1960, when the organisation approved a declaration stating that all countries had the right to self-determination. They won the case for Namibia at the International Court of Justice in 1971, when the ICJ ruled that South Africa was in illegal occupation of Namibia and that, until the Namibian people had elected their own government, the country was to come under the authority of the UN. South Africa contested this judgement.

After the Second World War, resistance flourished in many sectors of Namibian society, within church communities, trade unions, and nationalist movements. This book shows us some of this struggle, in the form of resistance in 1959 to the forcible removal of people to the designated townships of Katutura, on the outskirts of Windhoek. The doors of the houses in this township were marked with letters of the alphabet to show the ethnic group of the inhabitants (H for Herero, etc). There was a turning point in 1966 when the freedom movement started an armed struggle. After the ICJ judgement came from The Hague, this became a legitimate fight against an illegitimate oppressor, just as in Norway where Norwegian resistance fought against Nazi Germany during the Second World War. (When I began to show Namibians in exile around Oslo in the 1960s the "home front" was a natural subject to mention.)

The fight for freedom took a long time and took many lives in the process. Mama Penee and the rest of the Namibian population would have been spared much misery if many of the UN decisions had been followed up promptly. Instead, these decisions were sabotaged by the Western powers who held sway over the UN Security Council, and by the South African system of apartheid. The racist dictatorship in Pretoria was an ally of the West during the Cold War, an important supplier of uranium and other minerals, and many foreign companies became wealthy through the use of cheap labour there.

Namibia also had uranium and diamonds, but just as diamonds are forever, so it appeared was the imperial and racist regime. The occupying South African administration came under more and more pressure, both from more resolute opposition forces at home in South Africa, and military forces in Namibia and Angola. For the white South Africans there was no way back. They were forced to pull out of Namibia and Angola and enter into negotiations with Nelson Mandela and the ANC. After democratic elections in Namibia in November 1989, which ended with a landslide victory for SWAPO, Independence Day was celebrated on 21 March 1990.

Mama Penee never lived to see independence, but she would have been 97 years old. Her grandsons were there, however, and through this book, her life, thoughts and insights are conveyed.

There are victims who suffer dreadfully in this story, but when we reach the end of the book we realise that their sacrifice has not been in vain. Just as important is the fact that the genocide committed by the Germans never managed to eradicate the culture, language, religion and traditions of the Ovaherero. With indomitable strength they have survived, and their children and grandchildren are able to keep the values and memories alive in the present day.

There is an African saying that a lion hunter's story is never complete before the lion has had his say. This book by one of Mama Penee's grandsons is a tribute to that.

Tore Linné Eriksen,
historian, professor emeritus at Oslo Metropolitan
University and author of *The Political Economy of Namibia.
An annotated critical bibliography* (1991)

Preface and Acknowledgements

The motivation to pay attention to the history of my grandmother, Jahohora Petronella Inaavinuise, who came to be known as Mama Penee, started in 1952. It was the year the British King George VI died, which lead to his daughter Elizabeth becoming Queen of England. I was eleven years old, the same age as Mama Penee when she lost her parents. When I came home from school singing "God save our gracious Queen," instead of the "King", she asked me if I knew them. That lead to the question about what I was learning in "the white man's school". She then urged me to go back to school to learn and understand why the white people who were teaching us their Bible, came to kill, rob us of our lands and misuse women and children, if they believed in the same Bible? She told me to find out how that was possible, because if I failed to understand that contradiction, I could end up doing what the white people did.

I learned to pay attention to what I was being taught and to distinguish between assumptions and facts. When my teacher made me fail the final secondary school year because she said I was "very good at memorising instead of learning", I started to combine memorising and learning as tools to question and understand what I was reading. I also started to question my grandmother about everything she knew about her background, her life and her parents.

When I went into exile in 1964, I kept urging my two brothers to talk with Mama Penee about almost everything I was gathering in exile. They took notes of my questions and the answers Mama Penee gave them. The notes from my elder brother, Jesaiah Veroovandu Katjivena (1936–1991) were invaluable to this book. I am so grateful to him for his meticulous work. However, Mama Penee is the architect of this book, as she unknowingly sowed the seeds for it.

My grandmother's best friend Mukaatjauha, whose son was fathered by a German soldier; my mother's father Mateus Komomungondo; my grandfather Friedrich Kandukira, who became a priest as a way to escape being murdered by the Germans; his sister Mbakaa Katjivena, who also had a German father and who passed away recently; and Uncle Ramata Mutihu all had their own history of how they survived the genocide. They have all, in different ways, contributed to my memory. I am forever grateful for everything they shared.

Having been together in the struggle for the independence of Namibia for many years, I am grateful to Professor Dr Peter Katjavivi for writing about who I am, as he knows me. Very few people know me as well as Peter does. I am also very thankful to his wife, Jane Katjavivi, for having assisted me in various important ways throughout the writing of this book.

Over the years, many friends have been introduced to Mama Penee and my struggle to write her story. A special thanks goes to Arna Lie and her late husband Jan Erik Hallandvik for their support, advice and urging me to write about my grandmother and not about myself. Another such couple of supporting friends I want to thank are Tone Lindegaard and Per Tore Noddeland.

In searching for illustrations for the book, I am so grateful that my talented friend Morteza Amari could make a drawing from the only picture I have of my grandmother and one of how she may have looked as a young girl. I am also grateful to John Kinahan for the map which makes it clear for anyone to follow her footsteps.

During times when I was at a loss, Nishi Asdal was there to calm me down and urge me never to give up. She trusted me to do what I had to do. Our many years of working together made her know what to say that would make me do what had to be done.

Furthermore, I am so grateful to my family who stood by me through thick and thin during the process of working on the book *Mama Penee*. I profoundly thank my dear wife and life companion, Bente Pedersen, who never tired of urging me to finish the book, irrespective of my procrastinations. My children Ndukeimo (late), Kavazeua (in Namibia), Aicha (in Berlin), Ida and Nora (in Norway), and my grandchildren, kept on reminding me that the book I was working on was not for me but for them, who want and need to know about the great-grandmother they never met. Thank you all for the trust you put in me. My profound thanks go to Nora for the hard work of proof reading my English language.

I wholeheartedly thank Anne Marit, Amund and Asle Stalleland for the great work they did in translating the original manuscript into Norwegian. Your translation is so professional as if it was the original version of the book. Last but not the least, are two very professional people, both excellent in their respective fields. First, many thanks are due to Tore-Linné Eriksen for his excellent words in the Foreword. I thought that I had grown up with the few people who escaped the German genocide and should know more about it. Yet, the content in his book, *Det første folkemordet I det tjuende århundret Namibia 1903–1908* (*The first genocide in the twentieth century Namibia 1903–1908*), is the best chronicle done on the genocide period. I have read many books on genocide in different languages, and heard many stories told by the survivors of the genocide, but no factual testimony of that event surpassed Tore-Linné Eriksen's masterpiece. No wonder that the Foreword he has contributed to my book is so valuable for all those who need to understand what Von Trotha's Extermination Order meant. It is with gratitude that I thank him very much.

I am grateful to Jan Kløvstad of the Bokbyen (Norwegian Publishing House) for publishing the first edition of the book in Norwegian in 2017, and for agreeing to its revision and republication in Namibia by the University of Namibia Press.

I

Born to Survive

Sketch of Jahohora as a young girl by Morteza Amari.

1. The Tree of Origins

The eleven-year-old girl approached the cave where she and her parents were in hiding. A series of loud cracks rang out and she turned to see where they came from. She saw her parents fetching water from the river. A line of soldiers was coming towards them. She saw the soldiers lift their rifles and aim at her parents. They fired again and her parents collapsed on the ground. The soldiers cheered.

Almost as if she were sleep-walking, the girl went slowly towards the soldiers to embrace the same fate as her parents. As she got closer, she caught the eye of a young German soldier who stood a little apart from the others. Their eyes met, and with an almost indiscernible movement he waved his cap to indicate that she should leave, away from her parents, away from the soldiers. It was then that she realised that it was her destiny to live, and that she wanted to live.

This isn't the beginning of the story, although it is a deciding moment. The real story, as told by Mama Penee, began long before this happened:

"Not so far away from the origins of the mighty Okavango River, and closer to the oshana of the Aawambo (now called Etosha Pan), there is a hillock known as Okatundu ka Mbeti. Close to that hillock stood the mighty Omumborombonga tree (the Leadwood tree). According to Ovaherero mythology, the first ancestors came out of this massive tree. Their names were Kamangarunga and Musisi.

"As the first to emerge was the woman Kamangarunga, the women in the Ovaherero are traditionally the head of the family. After her, followed Musisi, who became the male ancestor. Kamangarunga and Mangundu gave birth to Kazu and Nangombe. Kazu was the original mother of the Ovaherero people and Nangombe was the original mother of the Aawambo people. Kazu married Ndeo.

"One afternoon Kazu and Ndeo went for a walk in the forest. It was a beautiful warm evening and they continued their walk until it became late. Instead of returning home, they decided to make a fire and spend the night there under the starlight. Whilst Ndeo was away gathering wood for the fire, a herd of cattle appeared. Kazu had never seen the likes of them before and was frightened by their appearance. As they continued grazing peacefully around her, however, she soon realized that the cattle meant her no harm.

"When Ndeo returned, Kazu told him what she had seen, but he was reluctant to believe her. Kazu took him by the hand and led him to the cattle. They were so tame that from that day on, the Ovaherero lived on cattle milk and meat. That is where the known expression comes from: '*Ozongombe za munikirwe i Kazu*' (cattle were first seen by Kazu.)

"Since then, the Ovaherero have been cattle herders, forever searching for better grazing areas to feed their cattle. Nangombe and her family remained in that area and started to cultivate the land. Gradually, in search of better farming lands, they moved into what became known as Owamboland, where they stayed. The name Owambo originated from the Otjiherero word *vaombo* which means 'they stayed' or 'they settled'."

Jahohora Inaavinuise Petronella of the Nderura mother clan, later to be known as Mama Penee, was born on 12 August 1893 in Omaruru. She was born at the time when the German Colonial Society of South West Africa (*Deutsche Kolonialgesellschaft für Südwestafrika* (DKGSWA), was selling all its mining rights in Okaoko to L. Hirsch and company. That was one of the reasons why Mama Penee's parents were saying to her that she was born at the time when land grabbers were selling our lands to other sneak-thieves who came to our country.

She was an alert girl with an enquiring mind, and a good listener. Already at the age of eight, she could recite the genealogy of her mother's line. Her grandmother, Kauatjitotje and her mother, Tutejuva, made her repeat the names of the family clan in a playful manner. She never forgot those names. She became proud of that knowledge of her mother's genealogy.

Her elder brother Eliphas Ramata Nderura was born in 1887 and died in 1963.

Traditionally, when the Ovaherero wished to know who you were, they did not ask for your name. They asked who you were. Giving only your name did not reveal who you were. A brief genealogy of your family, how you were born into that family and the place or area where you came from, said enough about who you were.

When the occasion was suitable, and time allowed, Mama Penee would start her recitation about who she was by telling the origin of the Ovaherero and of her family tree, depending on whom she introduced herself to. When she was questioned as to whom she was, she used to say the following:

"I am born in the Nderura omukwatjivi mother clan, the charitable mothers who could generously offer the needy anything requested except water. I am the daughter of Tutejuva and Mureti from Omaruru who vanished from this world in a matter of seconds. I was born to survive!"

Those who knew Mama Penee very well called her Jahohora, but hardly anyone did so. The name Jahohora was given to her by her parents at the ancestors' holy fire shortly after her birth. According to the Ovaherero tradition, the holy fire is solely the prerogative of the father's birth line. Her father was Mureti and her mother was Tuṯejuva, the daughter of Kauatjitotje and Mutihu.

Mama Penee's grandmother Kauatjitotje, her husband Mutihu, their daughter Tuṯejuva, and Mama Penee's father Mureti, belonged to a special group of people called the Ovatjurure, whose tradition was to help the maintenance of peace among families in the nearby homesteads and in the neighbouring villages. They were not medicine men or soothsayers. They served as advisers, urging those who came for advice to open their minds to peaceful solutions to their problems. As such, they never participated in disputes; they were looked upon as peacekeepers. This tradition was introduced to Mama Penee when she questioned her parents about the constant use of the word *ohange* (peace).

Ohange doesn't just mean peace. Its deeper meaning refers to something that ferments or germinates. This is to encourage the understanding that peace is not a static thing or in a passive state, but something which grows and develops over time. Peace, like love, is active.

The group's peacekeeping activities could be compared to a group of falcons soaring high in the sky in order to have a complete view of the landscape below them. They were brought up to have a complete view of the society they lived in. This didn't mean that they resolved every conflict they saw. Rather, people with disputes came to them. The various parties to a dispute would come for help to resolve their problems and reach reconciliation. This is the definition of the "peacekeepers" as told to Mama Penee as a child, and it always ended with the following verse:

Tji mwa kaengwango – hiyoo;
Twendee koya Nguvi – hiyoo;
Nguvi wa ri omutêna kwenûramwenu.

Are you troubled – yes;
Seek out the falcon – yes;
The falcon has always been and will always be your brother, your sister and your cousin.

The other saying that almost always followed this was:

Nokokure ku nowoye.

Wherever you are in the world you will find humanity.

In other words, wherever you are in the world, if you seek peace then you will find others who share your vision.

2. Inherited Peace and the Threat of War

1903 looked to be a peaceful year in the country. At the same time, there were rumours that war was imminent. Speculation about the possibility of armed conflict prompted Tuṯejuva (Jahohora's mother) to ask her if she understood the fundamental meaning of peace in spite of rising tensions in the country.

The German settlers were in the process of taking the land and the cattle from the Ovaherero. They claimed that the cattle had strayed onto "their" lands, giving them the right to keep the cattle. As the Ovaherero had no tradition of selling land, the Germans were in effect illegally confiscating the land, and the cattle that grazed there. It was as if the land rights automatically passed to the German settlers the moment they stepped foot in the country. Any attempts to resist this "confiscation" were met with arrests and flogging by the authorities and the settlers.

Jahohora understood peace to mean the absence of war but asked herself continually what she would do if war broke out. How could she hold her peace? To keep peace, it is necessary to understand the reasons for the conflict and to work towards finding a solution that ends in peace. It was becoming increasingly obvious that the Germans were not interested in peace or peaceful solutions. The only thing on their agenda was taking over the country for themselves. Many of the Ovaherero had organised themselves and were rising up against the German settlers in attempts to regain their land, and the situation was escalating. All attempts by the traditional chiefs to mediate with authorities to prevent the settlers taking what they wanted without consideration for the local inhabitants had failed, and outright war became inevitable.

Throughout all this, Jahohora was attempting to reach a deeper understanding of the philosophy of peace, and what it was to maintain an inner peace at all costs. There is no special method or system for attaining peace in a larger situation, especially if you are surrounded by war, so the only thing that can be done is to maintain this state of inner peace.

The future became more uncertain with each day that went by, so Jahohora's parents decided that in spite of her young age, as she had shown an understanding of the principles of peace and a maturity beyond her years, it was time to prepare her for her expected role as a peacemaker. Her grandmother Kauatjitotje and her mother also decided that although it was normally reserved for girls when they reach puberty, Jahohora should go through the rites of passage to become an adult. It was almost as if they foresaw the calamity that was about to befall the country and the Ovaherero.

At the tender age of ten, Jahohora was taken through the maturity ritual where girls were given their traditional head gear and garments to wear. They did this as a warming up to the real ceremony at a later stage. If the situation changed for the better, then she was to be given the full ceremony when she was the correct age. This warming up ceremony became very important to Jahohora in the next few years.

The ceremony was strictly in the women's domain and was kept secret from the men of the community. The girls were taken away from their homes for up to three days. What took place when they were away was never revealed and never spoken about to the men, but the change of behaviour in the girls when they returned to the village was visible. They acted in a grown-up way, as if they were mature women.

As the conflict with Germans increased in intensity, Jahohora never got to experience the full secret three-day maturity rituals. The only things she would later relate to her grandchildren were about what she was given to wear in her warming-up ceremony.

As a child Jahohora wore her hair unbraided, but as a growing girl and adult her long hair was threaded with colourful beads hanging down from her head. She was only allowed to try the ceremonial headgear that was meant to emphasize the transitional status of the rites. Her parents promised that she would get more to wear in due time.

She would recall what her parents had told her about the period of the year in which she was born, and the time of day. It was late afternoon when the sun was moving towards the embrace of the horizon. Stillness was drawing the sun towards its place of sleep. Her screams at birth were considered a call to the ancestors that their homestead was no longer depleted. In spite of this, she was given the name Jahohora which means "our village is depleted".

When Jahohora came home after going through the rituals, she was given a leather bag which, from that day on, she always carried over her shoulder. She never left home without it. The bag contained the jewellery and decorative pieces she had received at her initiation ceremony. Every time she was on her own, she would take everything out and dress herself in the contents of the bag: the belt and apron, and the ceremonial headdress were the most valuable things she owned.

Jahohora lived with her parents and brother and sisters in Omaruru, one of the first German colonial administration centres established in 1885. It was the hub of the German settlers until January 1904, when the war between the Ovaherero and the Germans began. Omaruru was one of the first places to witness the fighting, so her parents thought it wise to move to Omuramba-wa-Ndjou, now known as Kalkfeld. They divided up the family for safety, with the two boys being sent to families some distance away in Opuwo. Ramata, the eldest, was given strict instructions to look after his younger brother. Jahohora was to stay with her parents in their new home in Kalkfeld.

Jahohora's parents realized that conflict between the Ovaherero and the German settlers was becoming unavoidable. As guarantors of peace in their area, the family noticed that the interest in finding solutions was one-sided. The Ovaherero, according to their tradition, attempted to accept the German settlers as neighbours in order to settle the conflict in a neighbourly fashion. The Germans were only interested in signing what they called "Protection Treaties". But how could one be protected by the same people who had invaded your country by force?

Some of the Ovaherero chiefs were forced to sign the "Protection Treaties". Others refused to sign them. Chief Samuel Maharero of Okahandja and Chief Manasse Tjiseseta of Omaruru signed the "Protection Treaty".

The Germans started to impose borders that separated the land between what they said belonged to the settlers and what they said belonged to the indigenous people. The Ovambanderu chiefs Kahimemua and Kambahahiza did not sign "Protection Treaties", and they rebelled against the German imposition of power over the people. Both Kambahahiza and Kahimemua were taken as prisoners and executed in 1896. Chief Samuel Maharerero, Chief Manasse Tjiseseta and their followers did not react to the execution of their countrymen, and the split between the Ovaherero people became a reality.

It was then that Jahohora's parents realized that a peaceful solution was no longer possible. It became clear that the German settlers were sent to the country they called German South West Africa with the mission to settle. As far as they were concerned, the country came under the sovereignty of the German Kaiser Wilhelm, as allotted to them by the Berlin Conference of 1884.

And so it was that the parents of Jahohora, realizing the futility of seeking for peaceful solutions, moved away from Omaruru to Omuramba ua Ndjou, now Kalkfeld. It didn't take many months before they felt unsafe here too, so the family packed everything they could carry and went into hiding in the Okavaka Mountains, close to a dry riverbed. In this mountainous landscape they found a cave in which they hoped to be able to hide and live until the fighting was over.

3. When Fear isn't Enough

Jahohora lived with her parents in the small cave at Okavaka. They spent their time trying to find enough food to eat – berries, roots, small animals and, of course, water. They spent many hours trying to establish an overview of where there were water sources, and what other caves were close by, in order to hide if necessary when they were out foraging for food. They lived in constant fear of being discovered.

For her birthday, her parents gave her copper armbands, braided beads fashioned as a necklace to go around her neck and hang down over her chest, as well as *ozondao* (threaded dried seeds), also to be worn around her neck as traditional necklace.

One morning, a few days after she was given these presents marking her birthday, Jahohora went out early from the cave. As always, she took with her the leather bag containing all the ceremonial headdresses and other gifts, and she went for a walk. She was happily trying on all her finery when suddenly she heard the sound of loud cracks, like thunder echoing from cliff to cliff. Yet it was a cloudless morning.

She looked around and saw that the noise came from a group of German soldiers moving towards her parents, who were on their way to fetch water from a water hole they had dug in the sand of the dry river. They were equipped only with calabashes for carrying the water. They were not armed as they never carried arms. They didn't possess any sort of weapon with which to defend themselves.

Jahohora hid behind a bush, frightened and unable to move. More loud cracks rang out, and her mother and father collapsed to the ground. They hadn't even had the time to try to escape to safety.

The Germans – the killers – let out a cry of victory. They appeared happy with their actions. Jahohora couldn't understand. Her parents were not carrying weapons, they were not threatening anyone or anyone's property. They were peaceful people. Why should they be struck down in such a cruel manner?

Slowly the realisation of what had happened sank into her consciousness. She stood there alone, and somehow she understood what had happened. Her parents lay dead at the feet of the Okavaka Mountains, and she was totally alone. She was in shock and wandered without direction or purpose, as if sleep-walking. She was not even aware that she had started walking towards the soldiers, when she saw a young soldier wearing a cap with hair falling over his ears, his hair bleached white by the sun. He was already sweating in the early heat of the day and was in the process of relieving himself when she came into his view. His blue eyes watched Jahohora as if she was something of no consequence. His gun was hanging over his left shoulder. He looked at her but didn't say anything and they eyed each other in a challenging manner.

Then the soldier took off his cap and discreetly waved Jahohora away as if he were cooling himself. She thought he seemed so young, probably no more than 20 years old. The soldiers she had seen before had closely cropped hair but this young man had long hair, almost feminine in nature. She felt tempted to scream at him, but immediately realised the futility of such an act.

When she recounted the story of her survival in later years, Mama Penee would say:

"I remembered what my mother had told me many times. When Ndjambi gives you your life, it is given to you to look after it. Nobody else owns your life; you are obliged to keep it and remember that you are to be a mother one day. Never give your life away easily because you are obliged to give life to others. Preserve it, since it must have been meant to be." She thought, "If I was meant to live, then they couldn't kill me."

She was only eleven years old when this terrible tragedy took place.

K ATJIVENA

4. The Long Journey

Jahohora turned and walked away from the German soldiers without looking back, but the sounds of their triumphant laughter after the slaughter of her parents would haunt her for a long time.

She walked and walked until hunger, thirst, and pain in her feet made her barely conscious. She found some small bushes with wild berries, and luckily she knew which plants and tubers could give her precious liquid and nutrition. She was scared of leopards so, exhausted by the day's events, she finally climbed up into a tree. She tied herself fast to the branches to prevent herself from falling, using the leather items she had in her bag. Miraculously, she slept well that night. Every time she related that story to her grandchildren, though, they would howl with laughter, as the leopard is known to be a tree climber. In spite of this, she felt safer off the ground and in the arms of a tree at night.

Jahohora wandered aimlessly for days, until she lost all sense of time. Existing on what she could scavenge from the countryside, when she was lucky enough to come upon an ostrich egg, she ate well. She slept badly the following nights, her fear of the Germans crowding her mind. To make herself feel safer, she started to sleep with long sticks that she sharpened at the end with stones, to give her extra protection up in the trees when she tried to find rest.

The only focus to her existence was how to avoid the Germans. She was clear as to where she should not go, but she knew that wherever she decided to go it was unsafe. There were not many places where she could go and feel safe.

She had no idea that Germany had sent the notorious Lieutenant General von Trotha, to German South West Africa, as Namibia was referred to at that time. He arrived in the country on 11 June 1904. The German commanders had had no success against the tactics of the defending Ovaherero forces. So in August 1904, Von Trotha devised a strategy to encircle the Ovaherero troops on three sides. This would leave the Ovaherero troops only one way out of the encirclement at the Battle of Ohamakari at the Waterberg. They would have to go east into the Omaheke Desert. Von Trotha had also pre-empted the Ovaherero troops by poisoning some water-holes and by placing soldiers with machine guns at other watering places.

On the 2 October 1904 at Ozombu zOvindimba, von Trotha read out his infamous *Vernichtungsbefehl* (Extermination Order).[1] This order was written in the form of a letter to the Ovaherero nation. General von Trotha pronounced that they were no longer German subjects and must leave the country. He said that Ovaherero troops had killed and mutilated German soldiers and then were too cowardly to fight. If they did not leave, he would compel them to leave with the "long tube" (cannon). He would not spare any Ovaherero person, man, woman or child, found inside the German frontier. They would be fired at and driven away. He announced that whoever handed him one of the chiefs would be rewarded with 1,000 marks. The price on Samuel Maharero's head was 5,000 marks.

---

1 For the full transcript, see Hull, Isabel V. (2005). *Absolute Destruction: Military Culture and the Practices of War in Imperial Germany.* Ithaca: Cornell University Press.

Jahohora knew nothing of this. One day as she was walking, she was surprised by a German postman on a horse. The natural reaction for a child who had seen her parents shot and killed would have been to run away but she did not try to run. Instead she stood as if glued to the ground and watched the soldier approach her. He climbed off the horse and drew out a sword while walking towards her, his left hand holding the reins of the horse. He slowly pointed the sword towards her neck, and although she was only eleven years old, alone and unarmed, she didn't move but stood still and faced him without fear. He looked at her for what seemed like an eternity and she stared back at him with contempt. Finally, he said something, very softly, while putting his sword back in place. He shook his head and walked back to the horse. He took out his water bottle, drank a few sips, screwed the cork back on again and walked back to her. He pressed the bottle to her chest but she didn't react. She didn't move and the water bottle fell at her feet. The soldier turned and walked away, murmuring something she could not understand. He got back on his horse and rode away. Once she was on her own again she picked up the bottle, sat under a tree, and drank the water.

She wondered who these white people were, where they came from and why they were in her country. Why had this man been kind to her by giving her water? Why hadn't he killed her like the others had killed her parents? Why had that one soldier waved her away and given her the chance of life? Don't misunderstand, she had absolutely no feelings of gratefulness towards these Germans. When she later told the story to her grandchildren she always said that:

"I was in my country and I did nothing to anyone to deserve to be threatened, or to be saved, or to be forced to go hungry and thirsty by invaders in my country who turned out to be deadly assailants."

Jahohora became an expert at avoiding German army patrols. Her experience had taught her to remain alert to any movements or sounds around her. At the same time, her contempt for these intruders grew stronger and stronger. She trusted no one and became very good at coping on her own. She trapped rabbits and birds, found honey and ate berries. Occasionally, she did meet others who were also refugees in their own land, so she heard stories about what was happening. She heard that in some places Ovaherero were being forced to do hard labour, and she heard that women were being raped by German soldiers. She was determined never to be captured alive let alone to be raped. She felt safer alone than in a group.

Sometimes she would come to places where there were shiny bits of blue, white and green broken bottles, empty tins and unknown objects scattered over the veld. She learned to keep clear of these places. When she saw and heard vultures circling above, she knew that she had come to a place where other people had met the same fate as her parents. They had been killed and left for the vultures. Some nights she was lucky enough to find an abandoned hut belonging to Ovaherero farm workers, but she made sure that she left before sunrise so as not to risk being captured.

5. The Way to Survival

It was towards the end of December 1904 that Jahohora heard about von Trotha's Extermination Order. She heard stories about a strong man known as *omuzepe* (the killer), who was sent to the country. Other people on the run were talking about that man who had killed many people in Indo-China and Tanganyika. They speculated that the killer was in possession of magic and was thus invincible. Rumours spread that German soldiers would protect this man with their lives because it was believed that if he was killed, all the German troops would be annihilated. He was seen as not human but an animal whose existence was based only on killing people.

Jahohora listened to all the talk about this killer with sceptical curiosity. She wondered whom he was going to kill. Along the way, there seemed to be no more living people. She saw many dead people, or emaciated people who were dying, skeletons who were somehow still living. She gave General von Trotha the name *"Omukorokohe womaṱupa"*, which means "Bone cleaner" or "Skeleton killer".

As she continued her wanderings through the empty landscape, she saw more and more evidence of genocide. There were fresh graves everywhere; decomposed bodies of old people, children and cattle; and the bodies of Ovaherero soldiers who had been hung by their necks from branches of trees. The vultures were having feasts everywhere. She had never seen so many vultures before in her life. The thought of becoming a part of their feast only strengthened her resolve to survive.

She considered going to Otjimbingwe where the Ovaherero Chief Zeraeua had had an amicable relationship with the German missionaries and settlers before the war. In the meantime, however, diehard racists in Germany as well as the settlers in the country whose aim was subjugation of the Ovaherero, had turned Otjimbingwe into a war zone. According to them, the Ovaherero were inferior beings standing in the way of the superior folk deserving *lebensraum* – a living space. She heard about Reverend Kariko, a priest who was rumoured to assist destitute Ovaherero, and considered seeking his help, but he had also been arrested. The Germans had tried to hang him but the rope broke. The hangman took this as a sign that he was innocent. Kariko refused to accept the twisted logic of their mercy as they were continuing to kill his people. Why should he be found innocent when he represented the same rights as all the others? He was eventually executed by firing squad.

All the areas where Jahohora hoped to get protection had already experienced the deadly effects of von Trotha's edict: people were being killed, women raped, and lands confiscated. She decided to take the long journey to Otjaheundu, now known as Khorixas, which was inhabited by the Damara who were not at war with the Germans. This appeared to be the safest alternative. She would later tell her grandchildren:

"I was resolved to reach Otjaheundu. I was not aware that the place had three different names. I was lucky enough to meet with some other lost souls. From them I got information that the place I wanted to go to was also known as Ombuangonde in the Otjiherero language, and

Khorixas in the Damara language. That piece of information was vital to me.

"On my way between Kalkfeld district and Otjomumbonde, I again found fields full of blue, white and green broken glasses, extinguished fire places, empty tins and an assortment of unknown objects discarded over a large area. I found out later that those were the German soldiers' resting camps on their way from Swakopmund to Waterberg. I had to walk long distances around these rest camps to avoid walking on broken glass and the debris of strange objects. After all, the only sandals I had would have been cut to pieces if I dared walk over those areas.

"During the long walk, I passed through Okarumue, Oviraura, Omukandi, Epopo and Okaseraue. The village of Okaseraue was nearly untouched by war then. The Ovaherero there told me that I was a bit off course but not by too much. I may have to walk a bit longer than the short-cut but that road was much safer than the shorter one.

"From there I was accompanied and directed to Okatjondjoura by a young Omuherero boy a bit older than me. He was ordered by the elders to help show me the way. At long last when I reached Khorixas, it was April 1905. It was terribly cold and I was really lucky to have reached my destination before the start of winter. The people at Khorixas were very good to me. They took me to their Chief who took me in as his granddaughter."

6. Pleasantness

At the age of twelve, Jahohora settled down amongst the Damara people. They were very kind to her, and due to her small stature, she was taken to be younger than she really was. She remembered well these times of safety.

"Other girls of my age were more developed than I was. I had hardly developed breasts at all. Although the Germans had established some administration and a semblance of control of the area, I was never suspected of not being a Damara, even when the registration ordinance was introduced.

"I was the grandchild of the Damara Chief, but I knew that if it was known that he was hiding me, it would cost him his life. He advised me that if I was ever discovered I must say that I was captured by the Chief as his slave when I lost my parents. I kept that uppermost in my mind. I was supposed to keep it simple and innocent. I was only to be known as Petronella.

"One summer day we were playing *onyune*, which means pleasantness. *Onyune* is a game with 36 small round stones in 48 shallow holes. It is a mathematical game where one has to calculate the opponent's moves and your attacking strategy to capture the opponent's stones. The side that takes most or part of the opponent's stones wins.

"On that day I was completely lost in the game and was not aware of the commotion in the village. Suddenly, I heard a voice calling me to hurry to the Chief without delay. I was petrified as I ran to the Chief's home. Beside the Chief sat an African man who was dressed in European clothes and wearing a hat. I sat down beside the Chief in a traditional way, as a child was supposed to behave before the elders.

"There was total silence until the visiting man talked in whispers to the Chief who commanded someone else to bring drinking water. The wooden cup with water was handed over to the stranger who gestured to me to come and sit by his side. When I settled beside him, he knelt beside me, and taking the water in his mouth he sprayed it right in my face. It was so unexpected that I lost my breath for a moment. But I just couldn't help but feel amazingly happy.

"The man looked at me murmuring something I could hardly catch. When he finished with his murmurings he said, "Jahohora, my child, come closer." Yet it was him who was moving closer to me. He placed his two hands over my cheeks and pressed my forehead against his. I knew that this man was family but who was he? I knew him from nowhere, but he seemed familiar. I could see that he was full of emotion and could hardly speak for some time. He was caressing my cheek all the time in silence. He then said, "Jahohora, child of Nḓerura, child of the departed Tuṯejuva, I am your great uncle Kaṯunu, the youngest brother of your grandmother, Kauatjitotje.

"I was dumbfounded. How had he traced me to Khorixas? I wondered. Uncle Kaṯunu was first forcibly deported to work for the construction of the railway line between Swakopmund and Tsumeb without compensation. They were all prisoners of war who were forced to work from dawn to dusk. Many died of starvation and exhaustion but, miraculously, he had survived. He was later made to be a cook for the other prisoners. In the end, he was sent to work at a farm near Otavi for one of the German leaders of the *Otavi Minen-Gesellschaft*, who was compensated with a big piece of land for his military service and for becoming a settler. The farm was known as Omutjirauondjimba, which the Germans could hardly pronounce. I heard later that as many as over 900 men, 700 women and 600 children were sent there to work.

"I thanked the Damara chief profusely for the shelter they had given me, said goodbye to my new family and travelled to Otavi with my uncle."

In the summer of 1907, Uncle Kaṯunu died unexpectedly when Jahohora was fourteen years old. Luckily, the Ovaherero are a matrilineal society, which means that no child should ever be left alone without family. It is believed that as a child was born into a family by a mother, no human born of a mother could ever be alone. That was why the expression *Kwa riri nyoko keva ko* is used ('be alert when a mother cries'). At every death it is assumed that a mother cries. When Uncle Kaṯunu died, his sisters Katueumuna and Inaautepeho became mothers to Jahohora. This supported the belief that the mother line never ends. Everyone has a mother somewhere, even if they don't realise it.

7. Humiliation at Work

Under the colonial administration, people were forced to work wherever the German military or the administration wanted. Jahohora was no exception and she was taken to a German farm to work. She never forgot the great humiliation that she experienced the very first day. She was unceremoniously dumped at a farm without any instructions as to where she should go, or whom she should talk to. A man in a military truck drove her there and then just turned and drove away. She stood there in the sun for a while and then found a tree and sat down in the shade. She told her grandchildren about the experience:

"I was still wearing the remains of the traditional leather attire I had used through all those years I was a destitute. The most precious thing was the ceremonial headgear which I had received from my parents, even though I was not considered mature enough.

"Then a woman called Katrina came to me. She originated from the Cape and served as a translator – she spoke more than four languages. Her main work at the farm was the running of the kitchen, cleaning the house and looking after the children. She came to me and told me that *Frau* Kirschner wanted to see me. I followed her to the big house where the German woman was standing at the entrance to the veranda.

"*Frau* Kirschner waved Katrina away and started to walk slowly towards me. Her eyes didn't waver as they stared into mine. She was taller and bigger than me, taller but not fat. She came so close to me that I had to look up to hold her stare. For a moment she looked so hostile that I thought she was going to hit me, but nothing happened.

"I was about to smile but I knew that would only provoke her, so I forced myself to be calm while meeting her eyes without wavering. I could see that now she was close to tears and I felt sorry for her, when she abruptly turned around and walked away with quick short steps. I was left standing there wondering what really had just happened. I felt as if we had been fighting for something, but I had no idea what that was about. She had walked away as if she had lost the fight? But why?

"Later, towards the evening, the man who brought me in the military truck returned. I was again called to the big house. The man was sitting in a chair on the veranda and Katrina who fetched me was asked to translate for me. He had something very important to say to me and to give me some advice. He said the following:

"'You were disrespectful to my wife and I warn you never to be disrespectful to her again. You do what she says and you do it as quickly as she wants you to do it. Your job is to do all the washing and clean the yard; you will be taught how to wash and iron the clothes. Other tasks you have to do, my wife will instruct you. Now listen carefully. Right now I'm using words to explain how you are to behave. The next time I hear that you have misbehaved, you'll get a thorough beating with this.'

"He took a cane and hit the air with it to show what would to happen to me. Then he said: 'If I ever hear again that you have disobeyed her or behaved insolently, then I will have to separate your head from your body.' He used a sweeping motion of his hand as if he was cutting his throat with a knife.

"I automatically put both hands around my neck, and he said that I had understood the message because I would never find my neck when he was finished with me. He leant back a little in his chair before continuing. 'Those skins you cover yourself with will never be allowed to enter this house, nor do I want to see you wearing them again. Understand?' I nodded. I was dismissed.

"When I went to bed that night, I puzzled over how I had been disobedient towards his wife. We did not speak to each other; we just stared at each other. I hadn't even started to work for her so how I could have been disobedient was a mystery to me.

"At dawn the next day I was ordered to the main house. The German woman had heated water in a big iron cauldron. The warm water was then poured into a metal tub and with a pair of scissors the woman cut all the clothes off my body and ordered me to wash myself in the soapy warm water. We had no common language but her body language was easy to understand. Not a single word was uttered. We could have used our hands, mimicry and signs to try to understand each other, but I knew that saying something might be used against me as disobeying her."

Jahohora was forced to take off her headgear, which traditionally would have been removed only in a ceremonial act officiated by her parents or appointed relatives. She moaned her tragedy in silence as the German woman also cut her headgear into pieces and put all the pieces in the fire. She did not cry, but she felt terribly humiliated. That headgear was the last visible connection with her parents. She was devastated by it being destroyed in such a brutal manner.

After she had washed herself thoroughly, Jahohora was commanded to stand naked in the sun until she was dry. She was shamed by this, but it was far less of a humiliation than being robbed of her headgear. When she was dry enough she was dressed in a German Victorian style dress that made her move clumsily. She felt uncomfortable, and very hot, but she soon adapted as had the other Ovaherero women on the farm. This was the beginning of a new phase in her life.

"There were times when I felt sorry for that German woman," Jahohora would tell her grandchildren.

"She was constantly running everywhere, cooking food, making sure that the house, the garden, the whole farm, the children, the washing, the ironing, everything was done in an orderly fashion. That woman hardly sat down but kept shouting at the workers the whole day long.

"I couldn't understand why her husband working in the mines would eat three times every day plus the packet of sandwiches she made for him every morning. How could he need so much food? There were also things on the farm that fascinated me. One example was the pumps which drew water from underground and pumped it into reservoirs built for their drinking water. It seemed so simple.

"Everything seemed so easily available and handy but still these white people seemed restless and busy all day. They seemed to be more relaxed on Sundays when they had visitors whom they entertained with food and beer drinking. It seemed to me that Sunday and some Saturdays were the only times when I could hear them laughing."

She also described how she noticed that some young women even of her age were made to have children by German men, and told her grandchildren what she had done to avoid this fate.

"I made an oath that no German man would touch my body. I walked into the veld until I found a lot of nettles which I repeatedly rubbed on my arms and legs. The pain was excruciating but I repeatedly burned my body until the swellings started to show. I wouldn't tell my friends why I had the swellings, however often they asked me. I was happier that they thought I had some incurable disease that was possibly contagious. I never revealed my secret. That was how I got the nickname, Inaavinuise (larva mother, after the dead skin from which the larva would emerge). Not too surprisingly, the German men stayed away from me.

"I was given the name Petronella, which apparently means a rock, because I was as mute as a rock. I never spoke voluntarily, never volunteered any information about myself or my background to those with whom I worked. I was determined only to learn to do what was required, preferably in silence. After a while, *Frau* Kirschner started to become friendly towards me. We gradually developed a kind of friendship and she started to rely on me. If they were going somewhere they summoned Katrina and me in order to give us instructions about what we should supervise in their absence."

8. Mama Penee gets Married

In 1912, when she was 19 years old, Jahohora Inaavinuise Petronella, who came to be known as Mama Penee, an easier way of saying the longer 'Petronella', met Friedrich Kandukira, a young priest sent by the German missionaries to preach the gospel among the Ovaherero in Otavi and the surrounding farms. He was 25 years old. They married the same year, and a year later Uncle Willy was born on 11 October 1913 at Omutjirandjimba in Otavi district. He was baptised Willy Kandukira. Grandfather Friedrich was delighted by the new way of doing things, which included the practice that all children should be given their name when they were baptised.

Mama Penee disagreed strongly with her husband's eager adoption of the new ways so she named the boy Mbaamua which means "I was saved." It seemed meaningless to her that a European god would not approve of an Ovaherero name. Weren't their names good enough? She saw Christianity as a white man's religion, forced upon her people in an attempt to categorise and control them. Thanks to religion, and the names given at baptism, the Germans were able to differentiate between the black civilised Christians and "the rest".

The most painful thing about the baptism for Mama Penee was that as a compromise her husband gave the baby his great grandfather's surname, Kandukira. As she had lost all her family, the one thing she wished for more than anything was that the family name should carry on, so that one day they might discover other survivors that belonged to the Nderura clan. Her husband refused to change his mind, as it was the Christian tradition to carry the father's name down the line, and therefore to him this was the only thing that was right. He was also of the opinion that Mama Penee should abandon her vain hope that there were other survivors belonging to her family.

Shortly after Willy was born, the little family moved to the Okanjande Farm, where their second son Stefanus was born in 1916. In 1919, Mama Penee gave birth to her third son, Thomas, and in 1923 she had her only daughter, Musukomupe.

By this time they had moved to yet another farm taken by white settlers, and Mama Penee was growing weary of her husband's Christian ideas. She refused point blank to let him baptise her only daughter with the family name and threatened him with divorce if he should try. Friedrich was extremely stubborn and was convinced that women were put on earth to serve men, according to his interpretation of the Bible. At the same time, he realised that Mama Penee was prepared to do as she promised and he suggested a strange compromise – that instead all their children should bear his father's name, Katjivena.

Mama Penee reluctantly agreed to this compromise, but still divorced him later the same year. Even though they were divorced they had one child together in 1935 when Mama Penee was 43 years old. They called him Martin, and as with the others, he had Katjivena as his surname. Altogether there were five children as a result of Mama Penee's marriage to Grandfather Friedrich: four sons and one daughter.

Their only daughter Musukomupe, or Ruth as she was known, gave birth to her first child Jesaiah when she was only 13 years old. Ewald, her second son, was born five years later, and the third son Luther was born shortly before Ruth turned 20. When they were baptised, they were all given either Kandukira or Katjivena as a surname, but in their daily lives they used the Otjiherero names which Mama Penee had given them.

9. Settling in Okakarara

Those now called the Ovaherero are rumoured to have originated from the Lands of the Reeds which are believed to be in the regions around Abyssinia (today's Ethiopia). In their southerly migration they were stopped by the perennial Kunene River, (*okunene* denotes the right arm and means the direction to the right). This made them turn to the *okaoko*, meaning the left arm (in the left direction). Once they managed to bypass the Kunene River they became established in what is now known as Okaoko. Some settled in Okaoko, while others moved further south and split into various groups. Two of the rich Ovaherero *ovahona* (chiefs), Tjamuaha and Kahitjene, established their homestead in what they named Okahandja. Chief Zeraeua and his followers moved into Omaruru and Otjimbingwe in 1868, and the Kambazembi followed and built the first houses at Okakarara in Ohakaṋe in 1923.

Stephanus, the second son of Mama Penee and Friedrich Kandukira, settled in Okakarara in 1944, when he was 28 years old. He chose Okakarara because the South African administration in Namibia had designated it as the administrative centre of the area assigned to the Ovaherero. It wasn't long before the whole area around Okakarara became an Ovaherero reserve.

Over the first few years, Stephanus built himself a small house, three other simple dwellings, and some enclosures for cattle. When he was finally finished he went and fetched

Mama Penee and the rest of the family from the white-owned farm to install them in their new family home.

After many years of hard labour at farms owned by the German settlers, they had managed to save a little and acquire an ox, a wagon and several cattle. Now they could at last establish their own farm. However, the only route to Okakakara was unfortunately through an area occupied by settlers. Some of the farmers threatened to shoot them if they didn't leave their farms immediately, but others were friendly and offered them water for the family and their animals on their journey.

Mama Penee moved into the main hut that Stephanus had built. He had one that was a little apart from the others; Ruth took the last hut of the group, and the children moved into the hut in the middle. For the first time in her life, Mama Penee had a place she could call her own. Here she could live her own life, look after her cattle, and live independently with no white settlers telling her what and when to do things. Her grandsons could play wherever they wanted to without any white people restricting their activities and happiness.

However, Ruth worked for white farmers in the Otjiwarongo district, and her three boys were left in the care of their grandmother, Mama Penee, who became responsible for the larger part of their upbringing. She had a unique communication with her grandsons. She would begin a conversation by appearing to talk to herself and then suddenly, out of nowhere, ask the boys a difficult question they barely understood.

Every morning Mama Penee got up early and heated water in the three-legged iron pot over the fire. By the time the boys woke up, the water was boiling and she had already made tea. There was hardly anything to eat, so each of her grandsons got a mug of slightly sugared weak tea to which a few drops of goat milk were added. That was breakfast.

One of the advantages to moving to Okakarara was the Ongombombonde boarding school, then known as Waterberg Primary and Secondary Native School. The school was only 5 kilometres away, so the children could attend it and receive a proper education. The big disadvantage, though, was that everyone wishing to travel outside the "Reserve" needed a pass from the South African administration of the area.

Mama Penee had very few close friends. She kept herself to herself and was very selective even when she was friendly. She was a good listener and a person of few words, only contributing a few short, but wise and funny, sentences to the conversation. Her own childhood memories were limited to the relationships she had had with her immediate elders, and she treasured the things she had learned from them.

She remembered vividly the things her mother had talked about while they were out working together, or during the summer when they were collecting berries and digging for edible roots and bulbs. Although she became an orphan at the age of eleven, she never used the word "orphan" – a word she associated with defeat. Instead she talked of her mission in life as the building of a new family with her children and grandchildren. When the grandchildren asked her to talk about her parents, she half-jokingly responded:

"Am I not parent enough for you, my dear family? Do you really need to exhume my parents from their grave now that they are enjoying an everlasting rest?"

The only time she would talk properly about her own parents was when she was reciting her family tree or when she was persuaded to talk about the mayhem the Germans created in what they called German South West Africa. Sometimes out of the blue, she talked about having raised the families of the murderers. She cleaned their houses, cooked for them and washed and ironed their clothes. In spite of this she didn't appear bitter.

"I fed my own family with the remains of their meals, their used clothes, shoes, and household utensils that they no longer needed," she would say.

"It wasn't possible to live on the meagre salary which they gave me. To tell you the truth, the German colonisers owned us. They held the key to our lives. If a white person employed you, it was in exchange for your life. If you had no employment you were a vagabond, either to be killed on sight or to be sent to the concentration camps in Lüderitz Bay to work on the railways. People died there of malnutrition and constant inhuman working conditions."

She had been a destitute child roaming the devastated landscape, directionless, when the Germans were killing people. It was only by sheer luck that she survived the genocide. When she talked about it, she used to start by saying:

"What I have seen and experienced during that time, is like the phenomenon only seen by 'Nganja in the rustlings!'"

This expression, inspired by the wonder of rustling, or movement, in the mud, of a fish burying itself to survive the long dry season, was only referred to about things beyond known reality, things completely out of this world.

Mama Penee lived independently and alone with her grandsons. Ruth struggled to make ends meet in Otjiwarongo working for a number of white families. Mama Penee couldn't convince her that doing such work was denigrating. She tried to convince her that she would never make a decent life out of that employment, which was more or less equal to slavery. She was very saddened when Ruth died mysteriously aged only 42 years old. She had spent more of her life looking after other people's children than she had caring for her own. Her youngest son, Luther, was 23 years old when his mother died, and although he had missed her growing up, he understood that her sacrifice had been necessary to provide for him and his brothers. Mama Penee was 73 years old when she experienced the loss of her daughter, a grief she would carry with her for the rest of her life.

II

Challenging Power

Sketch of Mama Penee in later life by Morteza Amari.

1. When the Beat Changes, so Does the Dance

Compared to the average Omuherero woman, Mama Penee was considered short as she was only 168 cm tall. In spite of this, she would always stand her ground, however bad the odds were. She had good health and was always very active. At the same time, she never appeared to be stressed, or in any way affected by her hectic lifestyle, looking after the four children, the cattle and the household. She was loyal, trustworthy and extremely honest. She was also stubborn: when she had decided upon something she refused to change her point of view.

Mama Penee disliked any form of domination. She disliked it when she realised that women were obliged to cook for men, wash, iron, mend their clothes, milk the cows, clean the house and sweep the yards, while the men mostly did little or nothing. Her children and grandchildren were all boys apart from her one daughter. So Mama Penee made sure that her sons and grandsons were raised to be competent in all they had to do, in order never to have to depend on women to do their work, or ultimately for their survival.

There were moments when Mama Penee refused to do certain things and declined to explain the reasons for her refusal. She had been responsible for herself from an early age, and she didn't like to explain her reasons behind her actions, or lack of them. She was equally difficult regarding her whereabouts, where she was going or when she would come back.

She knew that there was always the possibility of a conflict situation just around the corner when she would be impelled to speak her mind, and at the same time she would have to be careful as to what she said and did. So she regularly whispered the following prayer to herself:

Ongumbiro yOvaherero ku Ndjambi Karunga
Ndjambi weyuru yambeka eke roye komeho wandje
Kutja avihe mbi me munu vi rire oviwa.
Suvira ombepo yoye motjinyo tjandje kutja mbi me hungire
  avi ha eta ouvi.
Hokora ena roye momatwi wandje kutja avihe mbi me zuu
  vi porise omuinyo wandje.
Kutja tji wa isana, omuinyo wandje u ye kove otja omukohoke
nu omutarazu tjimuna ombura ndji u hinda moruteṇi
rwombura.

Unquestionable Ndjambi
Creator of all things in Heaven and on Earth,
Place Thy hand across my eyes so that
I may see only wellness.
Breathe Thy breath upon my lips so that
I may speak no wickedness.
Whisper Thy name in my ears so that
What I hear will soothe my soul.
For when my soul comes to Thee,
It must come as clean and fresh
As the rain Thou send in the spring of the year.

This prayer accompanied Mama Penee throughout her difficult years and the rest of her life. It was a prayer that was passed down from generation to generation by the Ovaherero of Namibia. The god of the Ovaherero, known as

Ndjambi, was referred to as Ndjambi Karunga (the Merger/the Fixer), Kapurua (the Unquestionable), Kaheua (the Unpronounceable), Nguvitjita (the Creator), or Kamunika (the Invisible). Ndjambi is the embodiment of all the peacefulness that exists in the Ovaherero cultural tradition. The name Ndjambi was not used lightly. Nobody was supposed to speak Ndjambi's name out loud and no one was to speak of Ndjambi on behalf of another.

2. "What Did You Learn at School Today?"

When the British King George died on 6 February 1952, his eldest daughter Elizabeth, born on 21 April 1926, succeeded to the throne. She was crowned on 2 June 1953, when she was just 27 years old. This became an important subject at the school Mama Penee's grandsons attended, although the boys never quite knew whether it was a vital part of their curriculum or just a subject that the teachers were particularly interested in and keen to share their personal knowledge of. After a while, the children were made to practice the British National Anthem during lessons, the most important thing to remember being that they should sing "God save our gracious Queen" instead of "God save our Gracious King".

The next weekend the boys came home to Mama Penee and performed the anthem with gusto. They had no idea what they were singing. It was only when she started to ask them questions that they realised they been subjugated by the British, who in 1919 had given their mandate over Namibia to South Africa, to be administered by them.

Queen Elizabeth was three years younger than Musukomupe Ruth, the daughter of Mama Penee, who had been born in 1923.

"My children, do please come here and tell me what you are singing all day long," Mama Penee asked them. They meekly approached her but stood a metre or so away from her. She spread out the skirts of her long dress on the grass where she sat and patted them to indicate that the boys should come and sit down beside her. Luther took the invitation and cuddled up to her.

"Queen Elizabeth has become the queen of the British Empire after her father King George VI died. She's very young, three years younger than our mother. At school we are taught to sing about her but not about her father any longer," the boys said excitedly.

"Why do you have to sing about her or her father? What have they got to do with you?" Mama Penee asked.

The boys were proud that for once they had a chance to teach their grandmother something she didn't know. No one had asked them before about what they learned at school besides reading, writing and arithmetic.

"Our country is a part of the British Empire," said Jesaiah. "That's the reason why we have to sing about her like all the other countries owing allegiance to her."

"That's all well and good," replied Mama Penee. "But have you learnt anything of real importance at school? Something that means something to us in our daily lives? I've noticed that since you started school you have stopped using the word 'learning' but instead use the phrase 'being taught'. You know that the way we learn in our tradition is in order to sharpen our minds. What you tell me sounds as if you are spoon-fed knowledge at school."

Her voice was very soft but the questions confused her grandsons. They looked at each other uncertainly with lumps in their throats, and they were close to tears. She was asking challenging questions of a sort they never heard from the teachers at school. Out of desperation, one of them said, "We learn about the Ten Commandments." Mama Penee's face remained the same and she asked the next question in the same quiet way: "What do the Ten Commandments say?"

The boys quickly recited the Ten Commandments to her. She nodded slowly, paused in thought for a moment and then said:

"And as the white men gave us the Ten Commandments, are they only meant for us? Because if not, how could they come to our country, kill us, misuse our women and even kill our children, our men, and take the country from us? How could they could have done that and then continue to talk about the Ten Commandments?"

By now the boys were so frustrated and saddened that they really began to cry. They couldn't hold back the tears any longer. They felt both humbled and irritated as it had been Mama Penee's decision to send them to the school in the first place. Still sobbing, Ewald retorted with, "I am no longer going to that white man's school!"

Mama Penee remained very calm as if she was oblivious to their emotions and as if the issues were of no real importance. For the first time during this whole conversation, she smiled a little. "Now, for the first time you have said something I consider really silly," she said.

"But Mama what should we do? What is right for us to do?" the boys asked. They were desperate to do the right thing.

"My boys, sometimes in life there can be things which are wrong, but we cannot make things right because we don't have the key to what is right. Imagine that you are locked out of your house because someone has stolen the key, and that person who stole the key has no intention of returning it to you. What do you do? You make a new key because it's your house and your right to open the door.

"Now, when you go back to school on Monday, you will learn to understand how it was possible that the people who hold the key to the Ten Commandments are the same that committed those atrocities against us. Once you understand that, you will have the key to your door and to the path through your life. You may not understand all this now but if you remember it, you will have your future made, not in the way they want you to believe but in your own way. Never allow someone consumed by power to make you live your life as they wish you to."

3. Snakes and White Cattle

On a very hot October day, Mama Penee was sitting in the shade under the make-shift shelter beside her hut. The grandsons came running back from playing in the river bed. The earth was literally cooking from the heat and they felt their feet were on fire. They were sweating and felt relieved when they collapsed in the shade under the roof beside their grandmother.

While trying to catch their breath, one child started telling his grandmother about how he pitied the poor white children they had met at the river. Before he had managed to complete his sentence, he started another one, complaining that he was very hungry as the only nourishment they had had that day was the tea at breakfast time. Mama Penee shook her head and told them that they were the only living things hunting for food in this terrible heat, yet at the same time they were showing pity for the people who were responsible for their hunger.

It was quiet for a moment, then one of the boys said that she was wrong, because however hot it was the snakes would always hunt. Mama Penee told the boys to run over to the neighbouring tree that had a little shade and wait there until she called them. She stood up, went into her hut and came out again with a strip of dried meat. She said that if they wanted the meat they had to crawl back to her on their bellies, just like snakes. Driven by hunger, the boys attempted to crawl back to her but had to give up almost immediately their bodies touched the sand, because the heat from the ground was so extreme. They jumped up and ran the few feet back to where she sat. When they tried to snatch the dried meat out of her hand, she moved her hand away from them while asking if they still believed that snakes could hunt in such heat.

In unison, the boys said they no longer thought so – it must be impossible to hunt in such a heat. "So you agree that you are the only living being hunting for food in this heat?" she asked. They immediately agreed that it must be as she said. They desperately wanted the meat but she asked one more question: "Have you ever talked to the snake about how it can survive in the heat?"

"No Mama, but we thought it could still bite in the shade," was their reply.

Mama Penee seemed unaware of the boys desperately eyeing the piece of meat as she explained to them that the shade was in fact the best area for snakes to hunt in. It waits for its prey to come into the shade and that is when it attacks.

"Have you ever wondered why we sweep the ground in front and around the huts in the mornings and evenings?" she asked. They said, "No".

"That is because snakes move while it's cool, either in the morning or evening when the earth is cooler. When it's hot they wait for their prey in the shade. Snakes also want shade in the bushes. Also they follow the mice who are hunting for food in the houses. When snakes crawl where we have swept and cleaned, we can see the tracks they have made. That is one of the main reasons why villagers sweep the grounds around the compounds twice a day.

"As for your sympathy for the poor white children, does that mean you admire the way the white people live? The white people in our country live well mostly because we help them to be rich with our cheap labour. To be able to live like they live, you either have to work hard for yourself or you employ other people whom you pay badly to work for your comfort. If you don't want to behave like the white people in our country, don't imitate their way or go running around feeling pity for their poor children whose condition might not be different from your own. Eat the piece of meat and reflect on your lot.

"Try to understand who you are and why you live the way you live, my children,' Mama Penee continued. People, 'white' or 'black', are not bad or poor because of the colour of their skin. Anyone who sets his mind on material gain can do it by stepping on others to get what he desires. Generally speaking, the white settlers are more focused on material gain than we are, and they can be more vicious if you try to stop them from getting what they want. They are never satisfied with only owning cattle, drinking milk or eating meat. They want more. Only white people work even when it's hot. They have no respect for the power of the sun. They work the whole day doing this and that. They 'milk' everything they can put their hands on."

She stopped abruptly and looked long and hard at the boys. Then without warning she started to intone the old rhyme which they had heard her sing many times.

Hiyoo Hiyoo indjee
kongombeombapa
ndjaendaohumangombe;
Etundukarin'omuriro;
EtundurooNauanga.

Hi! Hi!
Come, take note of the white cattle
invading our homestead,

extinguishing the ancestor's fire
ravaging the Nauanga homestead.

Mama Penee was right. The boys were too young to understand the significance of her words, but they remembered those words for many years and puzzled about them. Much later if they had problems directly caused by white people, they would remember the words to this rhyme.

Even in Okakarara where there were only a few white people at that time, there were many confrontations ending in defeat for black people. The rhyme was sung often even when they were not aware of what the words really meant.

4. The Power of Interpretation

Mama Penee often told her grandsons the stories her parents had told her. The one story she never forgot was about Ndjambi, the God of the Ovaherero. No other human being should stand between you and Ndjambi, she told the children. Ndjambi is unquestionable, invisible, and unfathomable. There can be no intermediary between you and Ndjambi.

Mama Penee often wondered how her grandsons would be able to deal with two different ideas of religion – the Ovaherero traditions and those which the missionaries were bringing with them from Europe. Growing up under racial domination in every aspect of life, it would be understandable if the boys were very confused. When she heard her grandsons being emotionally moved by the plight of poor white children without shoes, dressed in torn clothes and having to walk everywhere instead of being driven in cars, she questioned what they thought about their own situation. It wasn't any different from that of the white children they were sympathising with. They were learning both from school and through other experiences, that the black people lived one way, and that the white people lived another way, and they accepted it as the natural order of things.

Some of the German missionaries used to tell the black people in church the following story from the Bible (Genesis 9: 20–25):

[20]Noah began to be a man of the soil, and he planted a vineyard.[21] He drank of the wine and became drunk and lay uncovered in his tent.[22] And Ham, the father of Canaan, saw the nakedness of his father and told his two brothers outside. [23] Then Shem and Japheth took a garment, laid it on both their shoulders, and walked backward and covered the nakedness of their father. Their faces were turned backward, and they did not see their father's nakedness. [24] When Noah awoke from his wine and knew what his youngest son had done to him, [25] he said, "Cursed be Canaan; a servant of servants shall he be to his brothers."
(English Standard Version)

It was then concluded by most of the white priests, that Ham, who was cursed to be the slave of his brothers, was the original father of the black people. So it was stated that it was God's will that black people should serve white people. The boys never forgot this story.

Mama Penee did everything possible to make her children and grandsons understand that when someone repeatedly tells you who you were supposed to be or what your natural condition is, be aware that someone wants you to be the way he wants you to be for his own interests. She explained that the evil people do has nothing to do with the Bible but is a direct result of human weakness.

"We as people try to justify our evil doings by any means possible, including using the Bible," she said. "No person on earth is born wicked or evil. People are taught to be wicked. Fear can make us behave irrationally with panic and desperation, which again leads to frustration, a feeling of helplessness or aggression. Everyone can feel helpless from time to time.

"I remember when I was hiding in the mountains with my parents, I decided to take a short walk away from them. As I walked behind a rock I immediately realised that I had lost my way and had no idea where I was or how to get back to my parents. I was scared and stood still behind this huge rock getting more and more confused and helpless. I called to my mother again and again, shouting that I was lost. The echoes of my shouting just did more to make me panic as I felt totally alone. I stood there and cried.

"That panicky feeling is unexplainable and awful. I felt so helpless. Luckily my mother heard my cries for help and soon found me. I can't explain how happy I was to be found. After that incident, I started to look at the expression 'Mama' in a new way. I used to say to myself, *Mama ma ama* or *Mama ma yama*, which means 'Mama saves'."

The boys felt that Mama Penee had really saved them from a lot of emotional confusion. Throughout the rest of their lives they would never forget that they had managed to master the art of controlling the feeling of innate panic when confronted by a white person, or someone who wanted to control them and make them feel less than they were.

"Children, remember that the bad experience you meet in life in one way or another should give you strength to fight against that fear," Mama Penee told them. "Have you ever thought about those young German soldiers who came all the way from their far country? That they were afraid of us? Yes, they were, and because of that fear, they could justify killing the people they feared. Fear is never clever, but if you don't control it, it will make you do terrible things."

5. The Need to Know and Understand

All children are inquisitive. They want to know everything about the things they don't understand, "Why is it like that?" they ask. "Where does it come from?" "Why…..?" Mama Penee's grandsons were no exception to this rule but she never ridiculed them or made them feel stupid to ask such questions.

"Mama, what is wrong with us?" Ewald asked one day.

"I've never seen anything wrong with you but since you have asked, tell me what you think is wrong with you," Mama Penee responded, without even looking up at him or stopping what she was doing – cutting up an old piece of material into smaller pieces, which were going to be made into a patchwork dress.

"People here tell many bad things about the Damara Police and the Omuwambo man just because they are married to Ovaherero women. Does this mean that if an Omuherero goes and lives amongst the Aawambo or the Damara, they would also find something wrong with him?"

The boys liked both these men as they were friendly to children and nearly always smiling. Mama Penee continued with her work and answered in her usual quiet voice:

"Can it be that the only thing wrong with you is that your curiosity makes you listen to things not meant for your ears? I cannot believe that any grown-up person would have that kind of conversation with you."

"But Mama, when grown-ups talk to each other, they say that we should only be seen but not heard. Or we are constantly told to go somewhere else to play. We were only sitting there and heard them say all those bad things. We were afraid to stand up and move away from them because we thought they might say that we had been listening to their conversation. So we pretended that we were only playing and acted as if we did not exist or were listening to their stories. Was it wrong of us to have listened to them, Mama?"

Mama Penee put the cloth and the scissors down and gave the boys her full attention: "I'm glad about one thing and that is that you did not tell me who said what. It is never good behaviour to listen to other people's conversations that you know were not meant for you to hear. When you notice that things are being talked about that you shouldn't listen to, you should leave and find something else to do. You boys have started to collect clean animal bones in the fields which you sell to Mr Woods, the General Dealer. Go and do things like that instead."

The boys went off to search for bones, which they collected in order to earn some pocket money as, in those days, bones used to be ground and mixed with salt for cattle feed. When they came back from looking for bones, Mama Penee told them to come and sit with her. She had been thinking about their conversation earlier that day and had more to say.

"Boys, not all people behave in the same way. Sometimes we are good and sometimes we behave badly. If you become aware that your behaviour is not good enough then you should correct it. When you admit that you have done something wrong and correct your mistake, you grow as a person, you become more honest, fair, and strong. Sometimes people become envious of others and as a result lose control over the things they say. You know that in our language we often say that, 'It is always the child of another who makes the worst mischief.' Never allow yourselves to be the mischievous ones by listening to stories that were not meant for your ears."

Mama Penee resumed her work without another word but her grandsons sat there with confused looks on their faces. She saw that they were confused and said quietly:

"It's always easier to behave as most people wish. It takes courage to do what is right regardless of what others want you to do. Every person has the ability to know what is wrong and what is right. If you manage to differentiate between what is wrong and what is right, you become a balanced person.

"Another thing you have to understand is that we are all different, with different strengths and weaknesses. You have your strengths and I have mine, but mine may not be the same as yours. I have seen that you boys have other good talents. Last summer when I came down to you by the river, you were creating villages with people, cattle, horses and dogs, using only the mud. I was so surprised that you could make all that with your hands. I could never do that. Do you think I am stupid because I couldn't do that?"

"No Mama, we don't think you are stupid at all. You know so many things we don't know. We always run to you when we cannot solve problems. You know SO much," Jesaiah answered.

"No, my children, I just gave you an example of something you can do which I could never do. No one person knows everything, and no one can do everything. That is why we say, 'No one finger alone can pick up a louse.' Things work better when we put all our knowledge together and work as a team. We can achieve many good things if our intentions are mutually good. That's why we select some people as friends and not others."

6. Who is Hurt?

One exceptionally hot summer afternoon, everything was quiet except for the cicadas with their ear-splitting sounds vibrating through the air. When the sun began to go down in the west, the air became cooler. The cicadas went silent, apart from a few isolated insects whose lonely shrills were periodically answered by another, and eventually there was silence.

Mama Penee emerged from her hut and walked to the single shady tree by the huts. Full of laughter, the boys came running towards the tree where she settled down. They were grey from the water dam where they had been jumping in and out of the muddy water. Their legs and feet were caked with mud, and they were shining with sweat. As usual the boys were teasing Ewald. His big stomach, a formidable chest and thick bent legs made him look different from the other boys. He was a good target for the white visitors who wanted to make sketches of 'savage' black people. They were breathing heavily as they had been running.

"What is it my children?" Mama Penee asked the moment they threw themselves on the ground beside her, but not so close as to dirty her dress.

"At last I got hold of him and thoroughly beat him up. I don't think he will ever venture to tease me anymore," Ewald replied, gulping the air into his lungs.

"Who are you talking about?" she asked sternly.

"I'm talking about Kaaṯakuma who hit me with a stick in the stomach a few days ago."

"Did you hurt him?"

"Yes Mama."

"Now when you hurt him can you tell me who else beside him was hurt?"

"I only hurt him and no one else."

"If you hurt him, then someone who loves him must also have been hurt."

"Possibly his mother might feel hurt, yes."

"Who else must have been hurt? Name all the people who might have been hurt by your hurting him."

"I think that his father, brothers, sisters, grandparents might also have been hurt."

"And what do you think your family feels about what you have done? How do you think I feel?"

"Maybe you feel sad," Ewald said, now really ashamed and staring intensely at the ground, afraid to meet his grandmother's gaze.

"Can you imagine how many people you hurt just by bunching your fists and hitting Kaaṭakuma? Who do you think you are to hurt so many people?"

"I didn't mean to hurt so many other people. I only wanted him to stop hurting me and making a fool of me. He called me a wolf and said that he was a jackal outsmarting the stupid wolf."

"Now that you know you have hurt so many people that you had no intention of hurting, what are you going to do?"

"I think I should go to Kaaṭakuma's parents and ask them to forgive me for what I did to him."

"That sounds like a good idea," Mama Penee replied, and she looked at Ewald who was still gazing at the floor. She put her hand under his chin and forced him to look at her, giving him a stern but loving look.

That evening after the cattle had been milked, the calves suckled and separated from the mothers, Ewald got ready to go to Mama Emilie's house (Kaaṭakuma's grandmother), to apologise. He was surprised to see that Mama Penee was getting ready to go there with him. After the usual friendly greetings, he asked to talk to the whole family as they sat around the fire. He told them what had happened between him and Kaaṭakuma and apologised to the whole family, including Kaaṭakuma.

Mama Emilie said, "You two young men fought, which means Kaaṭakuma should also ask forgiveness from your family." This he did, and Mama Penee accepted his apology on behalf of the family. After that evening, the two boys (aged 12) never fought again and from that day on they became good friends.

When they returned home, Mama Penee started to laugh. Ewald asked her what she was laughing about. She told him:

"When you told me that Kaaṭakuma hit you in the stomach, I remember a story my grandmother, Kauatjitotje told me a long time ago about how people got stomachs – and that was the beginning of all conflicts. But you two young people seemed to have fought because of your stomach for completely different reasons."

"But Mama why is the stomach the reason for all conflict?" Ewald asked. Mama Penee refused to answer the question and replied that the story would wait for another day. But one by one the boys politely asked her to tell the story about the stomach, and rumours of the tale spread like wildfire.

7. The Fable about the Stomach

Mama Penee was quiet the whole day and put all her energy and attention into her daily chores. That evening she made a special meal of beans, boned meat for sauce and maize meal, which they ate by the fire. After dinner, Mama Penee washed the pots and plates, dried them and put them away. She came back to the fire where the boys were waiting for her and sat herself slowly down. She knew what they wanted to hear, so without saying anything she launched into the story:

"*Apehara* – Imagine!"

"A long, long time ago people did not have stomachs. They had no need for food or water. So people idled away their time as they had nothing to do. One day they encountered several stomachs creeping and crawling alone on the ground searching for things to eat and to drink.

'Who are you?' the stomachs asked.

'We are us,' the people replied.

"The stomachs looked suspiciously at the people and said: 'You seem to move around with ease; can't you pick us up so we can be spared this ordeal of crawling?'

"The people felt sorry for the stomachs and out of sympathy they picked up the stomachs, which attached themselves to the front of the upper bodies of the people. After a while the stomachs shouted, 'We're hungry!'

'What is hungry?' the people asked in confusion.

'Okay we can show you,' the stomachs replied. We will teach you what to search for and we will tell you what to do with what you collect.'

"The people thought it was fun, something new, and finally something to do.

"The stomachs pointed out to them what fruits to pick, what roots to dig and what to do with what they had collected. For the first time ever, the people started to use their mouth, their teeth, and their tongue to swallow what went into their mouths. They were amazed by the sensations, and the stomachs were pleased, but there was something missing. The stomachs then directed the people to the water and taught them how to drink. Yet another sensation!

"The people were delighted. They began to develop new needs, which led them to start hunting animals. They started to build things which made it possible for them to produce food and utensils to use for what they needed.

"The more things they needed, the more they started to disagree with each other. They started to develop feelings of jealousy and envy, which led to more disagreements and eventually to war.

"That, my boys, is what started every conflict in the world today. Everything started when the people felt sorry for the stomachs and tried to help them by attaching them to their bodies. That is the end of the story."

Everyone around the fire was silent, each deep in their own thoughts. At last Mama Penee said, "I have two more stories to tell you, stories which you will continue to think about long after you've heard them. They are not fables like the story of the stomach; they are stories about patches and grafting. Now it's late and time for bed. Sleep well!"

8. Patches

A few weeks later, Mama Penee called together all the young boys – her youngest son and her grandsons. She never forgot a promise, so it was now time for the next story.

"When the Germans stole our country from us, they also forced us to wear these long dresses. Eventually they stopped giving us these dresses and instead they opened shops selling the material we needed to make the dresses ourselves. We couldn't afford to buy the 10 to 12 yards of material needed to make one dress, so we started to buy various bits of materials, regardless of colour or pattern, and we started to patch the old dresses. In the end you couldn't identify the original colour of the dress because there were so many patches.

"The style of the dresses the Ovaherero women wear today was brought here by the Germans, but we've heard people say that Queen Victoria introduced the style. We have no idea really, and I'm not sure that we care. The real question is, are these patched forms of the dresses still German or are they ours?

"We started to discuss where our dresses originated from. Some argued that our original traditional clothing was made of leather and completely different from those brought by the Germans. Others argued that the way our dresses are fashioned today cannot be compared to what the Germans brought to our country. They were the same in some ways but with the patches they were different. We have made them our own."

9. Who Owns the Fruit?

"Let us now move to the third story," Mama Penee said to her grandsons.

"When I lived in Otavi, I carefully watched the German woman for whom I was working. When she took over the property, she found a young orange tree in her garden. One day she went to her German neighbours who had planted lemon and grapefruit trees. They gave her some cuttings from both trees, and she grafted the cuttings onto the orange tree. I was ordered to water the tree on specific days and with a specific amount of water. After some months, the orange tree produced three different types of fruit – oranges, lemons and grapefruits.

"If we say there was an agreement that the person who owned the land on which the orange tree was planted had the right to the oranges, who owned the lemons and the grapefruits?" Mama Penee asked.

The children were in agreement that the original owner who planted the tree would expect to get the oranges, but not the lemons and the grapefruits. Martin, Mama Penee's youngest son, who was also there, was of another opinion. He felt that every fruit growing on the original tree belonged to the original owner, as the agreement covered the ownership of the tree without considering what fruit it might produce.

Mama Penee listened for a while to the discussion before intervening.

"The Germans came and took our country by force. This means that we are still the original owners of the land. Are you arguing that when we eventually get our country back, the Germans should take all the things they built on our lands with them, or do the things they built on our lands belong to us?"

The debate went quiet. Now all the children agreed that the Germans didn't have the right to what they had built in Namibia. Then Mama Penee asked:

"If the Germans feel they have the right to what they built on our lands, don't you think that we'll end up in a dispute that could lead to another war? If such a situation develops into a conflict, how do you intend to solve the issue without going to war?"

Mama Penee's questions were so difficult to answer. When she realised that none of the boys could come up with an answer she turned to them and said:

"You keep on asking me questions as if you were incapable of finding answers to your own questions. You sit comfortably and don't seem prepared to think for yourselves and try and come up with answers.

"You know that in our language you only ask a question because you have something bothering you and you doubt that the answer you have thought of is the right one. When you ask a question it means that you have something to say. That is why the Otjiherero word for 'listen' (*puratena*) is composed of two different words, *'pura'* = ask, and *'tena'*= say.

"This means that before you ask a question you already have an idea about what you are asking. It is therefore very important that you explain what you already know and why you have come to the question you are about to ask, before you ask it.

"Always share the thoughts which have led to your asking what you are asking. By talking and asking, or asking and talking, you will be guided to listening. That is why I'm not fond of responding to your questions before we have reflected together on what has led to you asking me."

Mama Penee stood up, went into the hut and came out with a handful of salt.

"Do you like salt?" she asked them.

"Yes, Mama."

She looked at them and then offered the children some salt to eat.

"No Mama, I thought you meant salt in food," Luther replied.

"Do you consider my question about if you like salt to be fair?" she responded.

This question sounded tricky and the children were not sure how to answer it, but Luther understood what she was trying to say.

"If you had told me what you meant before you asked the question, I would have given you the right answer," he said. The children now realised what Mama Penee meant in relation to the term *puratena*.

"Just as the graft grows on the orange tree, the school grafts their ideas and expected behaviours on to you," she told them.

"At your school, the teachers can only teach you what is in the books, and these books are written by white people. The white people wrote those books with the aim of teaching you what was in their interests for you to learn. This was their way of telling you about your history and your way of life.

"It's hardly an unbiased presentation. It's a version where the white man is supreme. They dominate and are even prepared to kill you if you stand in their way of occupying the space they want.

"I'm convinced that at your school, you are not learning, but you are being taught. In our language learning means 'sharpening your mind' not just being fed by others. I think that if you want to be a balanced person, you should be able to see the difference between what is yours, and what is theirs."

10. The Languages God Speaks

It was midsummer. The sun had moved towards the west and the day began to cool down. A pleasant breeze was making it easier for everyone to breathe. Mama Penee sat under her favourite tree shaking the *ondukwa* (calabash), which she used to churn milk into butter. She pushed it rhythmically back and forth.

"Mama, can God speak all the languages in the whole world? If all the people in the world speak to God at the same time, how can God understand everything they're saying?" The boys asked the questions very quickly in case Mama Penee stopped them mid-sentence with a question of her own.

She stopped shaking the *ondukwa* for a moment and turned to the children. The sun was shining directly at her, so she covered her face with her hands and looked at the boys through half-shut eyes.

"You remember that day you came home with a flat carton and many small cut pieces in many different colours?" she asked them.

"You spent the whole day in my hut because you didn't want the wind to sweep those small pieces of paper away. It surprised me that even when I called you to come out and eat, you didn't come. That was extremely unusual for you, not to come running for food. You continued putting those small pictures together until all the pieces were in place.

"I had no idea what you were doing, until you carefully carried the board on which you had put all the pieces out of the hut. Those small pieces had become houses, people, horses, all in different colours. I could see a dog and green trees with flowers. I had never seen anything like it in my life, and you were so proud of what you had done. You had made pictures out of those small cut pieces.

"You ask me how God can understand all the languages in the world. I think that what you did helps to explain how God can understand all the languages at the same time. Maybe God sees the languages just like those pieces of papers you put together into one big picture. I think that's how God who created all the different languages can understand them, in the same way as all those small pieces you put together became a picture which God understands the meaning of."

11. Laundry

One spring afternoon, Mama Penee was washing all the clothes in the hut. It was no problem to dry the washing as the sun was shining, and after everything was dry she ironed everything with an iron filled with burning coals. When she had done with the ironing, she called the boys together and said, "From today on, you will have to learn to wash your own clothes. You have to iron them and mend them too when needed."

The boys looked at each other in surprise, well aware that Mama Penee usually had a purpose behind her words, but this time they couldn't see what it was. What was she trying to say to them? As if they had a common purpose, the boys walked away and sat in the afternoon sun behind their hut to talk. They couldn't accept what their grandmother expected from them.

"We are not girls," they argued. "We will not do girls' work. We are boys about to become men. We know no men in our country who do the laundry, that's what the women do. After all, when we get married, our wives will do that for us." When they had reached that conclusion, they forced Ewald, who was considered Mama Penee's favourite grandson, to go and convey the message to her.

Mama Penee listened quietly and then with a smile she said, "So, you boys take me for a fool to teach you to one day abuse other mother's daughters to do your work?" The boys did not catch the importance of the question. So, in a soft but cold voice, she said: "In the meantime, until you get married, who do you think is going to do your laundry?"

The boy hesitantly answered, "Me…..I think?"

"Now go and make sure that from now on you do as I say," she replied in the same soft, cold voice.

From that day on if the boys didn't wash their clothes properly, Mama Penee put them back in the water. If they didn't iron their clothes well enough, she sprinkled the clothes with water, crumpled them up and put them back on the makeshift ironing board. Nothing was said and they learnt to clean and iron their clothes!

12. The Taste of Sugar

One of the boys loved to eat sugar, and Mama Penee occasionally sent him to the General Store to buy sugar for her. Although the shop was only about one and a half kilometres away, Mama Penee was not fond of talking to the white people who owned the shop, so she preferred to send one of the boys.

Every time this particular boy came back with the sugar, half of it was eaten. Nevertheless, Mama Penee kept sending him to buy sugar. One day, she had visitors, so she said to the boy that under no circumstances should he eat any of the sugar, as she needed it all for baking and for the tea she was making.

"I promise I won't touch the sugar," the boy replied. He went to the shop, bought a bag of brown sugar, and started back. But the walk seemed long and the temptation was too great. Although he managed to resist for a while, the inevitable happened in the end, and he started to eat the sugar. By the time he returned, half the sugar was gone. He felt very ashamed and didn't know what to do. So he emptied the sugar onto his shirt, filled half the bag with sand, and then put the sugar back on top of the sand.

He gave the sugar to the Mama Penee, who delightedly exclaimed, "I'm surprised that you really didn't eat the sugar." It was too much for him. He started to cry and confessed to her what he had done.

"It would have been better if you'd eaten all the sugar," she said. "I cannot use sugar mixed with sand."

Mama Penee only ever talked to the boys. She never shouted at them, rebuked them harshly or spanked them, apart from one time. Jesaiah, the eldest grandson, had developed a habit of provoking her. Time and time again she told him not to do it. Then one day she told him in her usual calm voice that if he provoked her once more she would spank him. That was something the boys had never heard her say before. Jesaiah repeated the provocation, and so without saying a word, Mama Penee stood up and looked for a cane. When she found a suitable one, she walked calmly towards Jesaiah, who started to run away. She followed him. He ran and sat in the shade and as she got closer, he started running again. She followed him for four hours, until in the end he gave up and came to her. She thrashed him thoroughly. Mama Penee was consistent. She meant what she said.

The evening after Jesaiah had received his thrashing, Mama Penee assembled her children Stephanus, Thomas, and Martin, and her grandsons Jesaiah, Ewald and Luther. It was a full moon. They sat around the fire knowing that Mama Penee was upset. No one was used to seeing her with such a stern face; it usually meant that trouble was coming.

"I called you all here because I have something I want to tell you all. I detest having power over others. I don't like corporal punishment. You only punish someone physically if you want to gain power over them. I am the first to say it and I am the last person who has the need to punish anyone." She turned to her oldest son and said:

"Stephanus, I am aware that you are the only one in our family who uses corporal punishment on your children. I never punished you in that way, if you remember, it was your father who did that. What I did to Jesaiah today is something I detest very strongly. Yet Jesaiah, you seemed desperate to want someone to have power over you. You wanted to give me power over you by provoking me as you did today.

"Another one of you is also constantly eating the sugar. I ask you every time I send you to the shop not to eat it, but you do it anyway. You are begging for punishment. You are offering yourselves to me to hurt you.

"Have you ever thought about why you invite someone to hurt you? I believe you do that because you feel insufficient and your disobedience is a way of begging for someone to take power over you.

"I don't care if you understand this or not but you should never ever forget that if you allow someone to have power over you, you become a useful object-like thing. If the person who has power over you tells you that you are not going to be punished, that person is telling you that he or she has the 'right' to punish you or not to punish you. If you accept that, you should know that that person can use you in any way he or she wants. You have become a tool, a useful thing lacking its own will.

"From today on, you will stop inviting me to punish you and you will have to look at yourselves to develop characters that will not allow you to be the slave of someone else. Whatever someone demands of you or says about you, you should always remember that you know yourself better than the people who are talking about you. To know yourself means that you trust in the person you are and you are not afraid to be right. I am done now. You may all go, as I need some peace."

Solemnly, and without a word, they all went in different directions.

Mukaatjauha Magdalena Katjari and Mama Penee, close friends since childhood

13. Childhood Friends Come Face to Face

December 1959 was a tumultuous year for the inhabitants of the Old Location in Windhoek. The Africans were being moved by force to the new segregated Katutura Township. On 10 December, the day of the big demonstrations against these forced removals, children were sitting on stones in the front row of the demonstrating masses. There were hundreds of people there. Everybody was tired and hungry, but still determined to be full participants in the demonstration.

The tension in the crowds grew more intense and then, all of a sudden, the municipal police and some white volunteers opened fire on the crowd. People were frightened by the shooting and started running away. Ten people were killed that day and many others wounded. There were no African doctors to help the injured, only black nurses. Fortunately, one of them came to help all the injured.

Most of the children escaped injury, perhaps because they were sitting down. Many of them also ran for their lives and in some miraculous way they found each other again later. One had been shot in the arm, others had smaller injuries, several of them were crying. One bullet had gone through the fleshy part of the lower arm of one boy, but the nurse helped him.

Early one evening later that month, Mama Penee and her childhood friend, Mukaatjauha Magdalena Katjari, went to the forest to collect wood. The temperature was becoming cooler but they sat down to rest a bit before carrying the wood home. They were used to being quiet together.

"I understand your grandson escaped injury at the Windhoek Shootings," said Mukaatjauha in a wondering voice. "I believe we are meant to be alive for a reason." Silence followed before she continued and asked her friend a direct question:

"Inaavinuise, can you tell me, when you poisoned your skin to create all those wounds and pus, in order to keep the German men away, didn't it hurt a lot?"

For some reason, the question irritated Mama Penee. But the only indication of this was a briefly raised eyebrow that flittered for a second. Nothing more. She replied to Mukaatjauha in a calm voice:

"Maybe you can tell me that it didn't hurt when that German man made you pregnant? Did you let him rape you to save your life, or could you just not escape him?"

Mukaatjauha didn't take offence at Mama Penee's words. They knew each other very well. She responded in a calm voice:

"At that time it was not so easy to say if it was consensual or by force. Force was always there, as was my need to survive. I didn't know if I refused him, whether he would kill me or not. Killing was accepted by the administration at that time. I just let him do what he wanted to with me. Yes, the pain was in my heart. But today, I am at peace. I love my son, Tommy. Yet in all he does, he resembles his father."

Mukaatjauha could see that her friend was having difficulty in opening up. There was an uneasy silence for a time.

Mama Penee said in a tired soft voice:

"Yes, there was much pain in my heart too. I couldn't imagine a German man touching my body after what those men did to my family. I had to poison my body to prevent that. The alternative for me was to follow my family rather than to breed a German child.

"We must never forget those women who lost their minds and became disoriented because they had been abused, and had babies who were not their choice. They were mostly young girls who didn't realise what was being done to them.

"We should also think about those who were banned from the farms because the German wives couldn't stomach what their husbands had done to the black women working there. And some thoughts must also go to the German women who were helpless to control their husbands' bad behaviour.

"You and I were meant to survive in order to give new life to our almost destroyed nation. In a way we have to be thankful for what we have had to pay in order to remain alive. As we say, God is unquestionable because we are unable to perceive what awaits us or the purpose of why we were given life."

Mama Penee stood up, stretched out her hand to her friend, who took it and stood up too. They picked up their heavy loads of wood, balanced them on their heads, and walked home.

14. Deplorable Acts

In 1963, Mama Penee was informed by her youngest son and her three grandsons that they had made women pregnant without being married to them. She didn't like it at all. In accordance with tradition, the boys' parents had to go to the girls' parents and tell them of the pregnancy. This visit was taken as recognition of paternal responsibility for the unborn child.

The war had all but destroyed the Ovaherero and their traditions, but they had made an oath to rebuild the nation again. There were more women than men who had survived the war, and it was almost considered a civic duty to get as many women as possible pregnant.

Mama Penee dispatched Stephanus and Thomas to inform two of the affected families who lived in a village a few kilometres away. Martin was dispatched to Otuvingo to one family, and Stephanus to another. Mama Penee herself visited another set of parents in Okakarara. After the visits, when everything was settled and lamps had been given to the families as a symbol of the new links between them, she called all the boys to yet another meeting.

"I think we were lucky that all the parents of the girls accepted our recognition of your acts. You know that I don't approve of your behaviour, but I would like to talk to you about why this behaviour has become so common in our society.

"After the genocide of 1904–1908, the Ovaherero made an oath that they were going to rebuild the nation again. You must be aware that after the war, there were more women than men. You know that the Ovaherero women shy away from uncircumcised men, which has left their choice limited to the few surviving men. The consequences of this are that the men now have easy access to plenty of women. You are now beginning to adopt this attitude of 'one man, several women'.

"I can't stop you from behaving like this, but I want you to know why this loose behaviour has developed. I hope you will think about the parents of the girls, the girls you are involved with, and most importantly the unborn children, before you continue behaving in this manner. You must be aware that the children have to be looked after and be supported throughout their development into adults. Whatever you do, be responsible.

"I am so very grateful for having been allowed the opportunity to be your mother and grandmother. There was no way for me to know that you would be part of my life. Today, I'm going to talk like a preacher, something I'm not fond of. It can never be fair to you or to me, if I start to reveal to you what the core of my belief is.

"I've never talked to you about God or Ndjambi. In my tradition no one should be in a position to preach his belief in God to someone else without having assumed some kind of power over the other person. God or Ndjambi reveals Himself through all creation. There was a time when we were obliged to slaughter, hunt animals, or cut a tree or plant, but before we did that, we had to ask their spirits to forgive us by explaining the reason for doing what we were about to do.

"By my talking to you about Ndjambi I am violating that code. It is a name we only whisper to ourselves.

"Let's instead talk about our behaviour and the way it affects the world we live in, the world Ndjambi gave as a gift to all living beings.

"If a woman allows you to touch her, she has entrusted some of the most precious parts of herself to you to handle with care and respect. That woman has allowed you possibly to share a new life with her. What an enormous trust! That trust might result in many future generations you have no inkling of. The creation of Ndjambi could be in you and in her when you are united in love towards each other.

"I am not here to pass judgment on how you handle your relationships with the women you are involved with. I have noticed that not one of you asked me to ask the parents of those girls to honour them with a proposal of marriage. You behave as if the daughters of other mothers are there for your taking, without any sense of commitment on your part. In Otjiherero, we have that very revealing expression *Otjitona tja ya norutu* – 'Whatever part of the body or soul that was injured, has an effect on the rest of the body'. If you harm another person in whatever way, it is equal to poisoning that person. Exercising power over another person is a deplorable act which must be avoided by all means.

"I have talked far too much today but it is my prayer that whatever I have said today will not harm anyone. Ndjambi, breathe Thy breath upon my lips so that I may speak no wickedness."

It was raining heavily, and the sound of the rain drumming on the grass thatched roof of Mama Penee's hut lulled everyone into a semi-slumber. But despite the peaceful atmosphere in the village, talk of the genocide – *otjitiro otjindjandja* – prompted one of the grandsons to ask if there could be war again.

"I don't know for sure," Mama Penee replied. "But it's possible that there will always be war. As long as there are people who exercise power over others, the oppressed will sooner or later rebel against whoever oppresses them. It might take years but it will happen again. Wars take place all over the world, particularly in countries where people feel they are unjustly treated."

"But Mama, will people ever live together without fighting?" the boy asked wonderingly.

"I hope and believe it's possible for people to live together without going to war," said Mama Penee.

"It's only a matter of people realising that oppression has 'short legs'. Oppression doesn't last forever. Nothing lasts forever. If only everybody could understand that the world was given to all the people living in the world. When all the people in the world start to behave as if they are part of the same human body, they will know peace.

"The body has many different parts working in harmony. Every limb and organ has a function which coordinates with the other limbs and organs in the body. When all of us in the world find ourselves like parts of one body, we can find peace in the world.

"This may not happen in our lifetime, but if we all work to accept that we all belong to the same world, peace is possible. That's what I believe. That is my dream.

"I wonder what you young people dream about, or how you wish your world to be. You are the ones who go to school, read books, talk in foreign languages, and possibly look at the world with different eyes from mine. My world is about to end but yours is starting. I wish to believe that you have a better chance to communicate with the rest of the world."

She continued:

"Of course, the white people won't like the idea of you being their equals as long as you are there to make their lives easier and more profitable for them. They want you to accept the notion that you're not as good as they are. If you believe that they are better people than you, then nothing is going to change.

"Your behaviour is starting to worry me. When you start to look at women as people who should produce children for you but not as people with whom you have common purpose, how can you expect the whites to see you as equal to them? You seem to want the women to serve your interests without taking any responsibility for your actions.

"When you find a common purpose with the women, with the Aawambo, the Damara, the whites and all the other people you encounter, you might be on the way to change the world. You have to believe that, and behave with that in mind, then you might end up being the seed that becomes the tree bearing fruit. I have no more than that to say.

"First we may doubt what we are told, then gradually we start to get used to hearing something, until it becomes normal. The more people take something to be normal, the more we start to take it for granted. Eventually we start to believe in what we first doubted."

"The whites gave us this piece of land. They told us it was our land. We knew it was not ours but gradually we started to accept it as our land because we were left with no choice but to live here."

15. What is Freedom?

In 1952, when she was 59 years old, Mama Penee heard about a country somewhere in Africa being given freedom. She kept repeating the words "given freedom", over and over again.

Her grandsons were old enough also to be interested in the possibility of African freedom, and they talked to Mama Penee about the liberation of Ghana, the first African country to be given freedom by the British. However, Mama Penee did not trust a freedom given by whites or any conquerors.

"Children, you are the ones who are educated at school," she told them. "Can you tell me how a country which has been conquered can be handed back to the people it was taken from? In the first place, the whites must have used force to win the country. Why are they now giving it back?"

"The people of the Gold Coast, which is now Ghana, demanded their freedom back under the leadership of Kwame Nkrumah, and in the end the British gave the country back," replied one of the boys was now attending the Augustineum College in Okahandja. He explained in detail to Mama Penee the name of the Gold Coast, what it meant in Otjiherero, and where Kwame Nkrumah studied.

"He is a well-educated man just like the white people. He studied together with them. They respect him."

Her grandson was convinced that studying with the whites in their schools could give the black people the right to their freedom.

"Children, white people came to our countries for a reason," Mama Penee insisted. "They fought us and they won. They started to see our countries as their own. They built roads and houses. They worked on the land, owned farms and made their own type of administration. They created schools for their children and separate ones for our children. They taught our children how to behave and how to like what the white people had brought with them to our country. Their presence became normal the more their power became accepted.

"Of course, some of the educated blacks would like to have the same things that the whites have. Those blacks started to ask for freedom – the same freedom that the whites already had. Of course, they could have freedom and everyone could live in peace. We used to fight against other tribes. When we captured their fighters, we used to make them adopt our traditions, gave them cattle when they looked after our cattle, and gradually, they became part of our tribe. They helped to strengthen our power while helping us to become richer.

"The whites have realised that when the educated Africans started to think like them, wishing for the same things that whites had, they could be given freedom as this won't change white domination. I believe that is what the whites have done by giving the black people freedom. It is a freedom that won't put the white people in that country to any disadvantage."

Her grandson argued that the people of Ghana were given back the whole of their country:

"But Kwame Nkrumah has taken over the whole country, the Governor's Palace as well as the whole government. The people of Ghana have elected him as the President."

"What is the President?" asked Mama Penee. "Does that make him the Chief of the country? Was he born in the Chief's family?"

"No, Mama. He was selected by the people of the country because he was the best educated, and he peacefully led the demand for the freedom of the people of the country. The President is the head of the government and the country."

"So, the white people said, 'We have trained you well enough to be the chief and the people have accepted that,' so they gave the country back?" asked Mama Penee. "I only wonder what the whites are gaining by giving the country back. You said the country was called gold something, I presume it had gold. Did the whites give the gold back as well?"

"Mama, you don't understand," her grandson replied. "Ghana has gold, cocoa and many other things. The black people of Ghana now have the right to share the riches with the white people who have remained in the country after independence."

Mama Penee continued to challenge him.

"Doesn't that mean that the white people who remained in the country are welcoming the owners of the country to share their riches with them? So the white gains are not given back to the blacks. The whites have kept the riches and are now inviting the inhabitants of Ghana to share in their riches? That is what I suspected. The one who took the power away from you would never give back what he has taken by force, without knowing what he is gaining by giving back what he took by force in the first place. So they trained the man to behave in the way they wanted him to behave if he wanted to be the leader in the country. Whites are very sly. I cannot help wondering as to who is misleading whom."

"Mama, people fought long and hard to gain the freedom and they forced the whites to accept their right to freedom and they achieved it," her grandson insisted.

"I am starting to think that the more you continue to rub shoulders with the whites in their schools, the more you will start to think and behave like them," she said.

"When you are in harmony with their interests, you will accept whatever they offer you in your land. If you don't believe me, go to their country and start to behave the same way they behave in our countries. First, they will make sure that you behave according to the way they would like you to behave in their country. If you ignore that, they will harm you in any way they see fit.

"If an elephant steps on an ant, it doesn't notice that it has harmed something. We are like ants to them. Power becomes blind to all rules when it is challenged. It protects what it has gained. When I listen to you, I am convinced that we too are going to get the same type of freedom you are talking about. I am glad that I will no longer be around when that happens."

"Mama, what can we do to get our whole country back? Isn't it better to at least get a part of the country than nothing at all?" came the plea.

"I'm not saying one shouldn't accept limited freedom, but you should know what really hides in the bush before you venture into the bush. I told you some time ago that you should go back to school to learn to understand what moved the white people to undermine the good things they taught us in the Ten Commandments. When you understand that, you will surely know how to handle the power you cannot win over, and how to handle the limited power you might be given. You might also learn how to build on the limited power you get.

"The best would be if you can become so clever as to get the rest they still have, by using the rules they use in their own countries amongst themselves. Those whites who remain in the country and still have so much power, maybe you could invite them to be partners to bring about the changes you want for your country. If you understand the rules of power, you can survive in the same way as you would if you swam in rough water and knew the unpredictability of the currents."

16. Accepting the End of Life

When her grandsons became young men and moved away in 1958, Mama Penee was alone for some years. The only person who lived with her was Uncle Martin, who was also in many ways a lonesome person. He would refuse to talk to anyone for a week or two if he was in the mood to be alone.

Her grandsons were spread over some distance. Ewald was studying in Okahandja and the other two found work in Windhoek. After Stephanus bought a farm further away, her son Thomas came home to be with Mama Penee. A few years later, he too joined his brother on the farm, so the eldest grandson Jesaiah moved back to Okakarara to be with her. It was only when Jesaiah came back that the correspondence between Mama Penee and the other children started. She dictated her messages to them through him. Even when Ewald left the country to Tanganyika (now Tanzania), Egypt, Algeria, Belgium, Lusaka and Germany, and became part of the movement for independence, the correspondence continued. Luther went to Ongombombonde. Mama Penee's only daughter, Musukomupe Ruth, died in 1965.

Mama Penee strongly wished to know how her grandsons were doing wherever they were. Ewald, who was now living abroad, promised that to reassure her that he was fine, he would send her the type of material the Germans had brought to Namibia. This became popular among the Ovaherero women for making their long dresses, which nearly swept to the ground. The material was known as *Otjindoitji*, meaning German material, and it was no longer readily available in the country. Ewald searched for the material and found it in Berlin. He sent 12 metres of it to Mama Penee in June 1975. She felt reassured and was happy that all was well with him even though he was far away.

Martin became father to a baby girl, Kavetjipo, born on 4 December 1971. From the very start, she became her grandmother's darling. When she started walking, she became Mama Penee's walking companion.

For many years, Mama Penee had talked about how she wanted to meet her end. She wished to use her last energy to walk into the forest and die alone. She resented the idea that someone who knew nothing or had no connection with her spirit would close her eyes. Kavetjipo, whom she would have preferred to do that for her, was too little to perform such an act. So one day Mama Penee walked into the forest and died alone as she had wished. That was on 5 November 1975, when she was 82 years old.

Bibliography

Alnaes, K. (1981). Going through the War: Herero Women in Botswana. Paper presented at the ASAUK Symposium in African Politics, 22 September 1981.

Baer, E. (2017). *The Genocidal Gaze: From German South West Africa to the Third Reich*. Detroit: Wayne State University Press, 2017; Windhoek: University of Namibia Press, 2018.

Beer, G. L. (1923). *African Questions at the Paris Peace Conference*. New York: The Macmillan Company.

Bley, H. (1971). *South West Africa under German Rule, 1894–1914*. London: Heinemann.

Dierks, K. (2003). *Chronologie der Namibischen Geschichte*. Windhoek: Namibia Wissenschaftliche Gesellschaft.

Drechsler, H. (1980). *Let Us Die Fighting: the struggle of the Herero and Nama against German imperialism (1884–1915)*. London: Zed Press.

Erichsen, C. W. (2008). *'What the Elders used to say': Namibian Perspectives on the Last Decade of German Colonial Rule*. Windhoek: Namibia Institute for Democracy (NID) and the Namibian-German Foundation (NaDS).

Gewald, J.-B. (1998). *Herero Heroes: a socio-political history of the Herero of Namibia, 1890–1923*. Oxford: James Currey.

Hangara, N. (2017). *Otuzo twOvaherero*. Windhoek: University of Namibia Press.

Hess, Klaus A., & Becker, Klaus J. (2002). *Vom Schutzbebiet bis Namibia 2000*. Göttingen: Klaus Hess Verlag, Edition Namibia 7.

Hull, I. V. (2005). *Absolute Destruction: Military Culture and the Practices of War in Imperial Germany*. Ithaca: Cornell University Press. [For von Trotha's 1904 Extermination Order]

Kavari, J. U. (2001). Social Organisation, Religion and Cosmos of Ovaherero. *Journal of Religion and Theology in Namibia*, vol. 3(1), pp. 116 – 160 (EIN Publications).

Koessler, R. (2015). *Namibia and Germany: Negotiating the Past*. Windhoek: University of Namibia Press.

Kunene, M. (1982). *The Ancestors and the Sacred Mountain*. London: Heinemann Educational Books.

Mossolow, N. C. (1975). *Waterberg. Beitrag zur Geschichte der Missionsstation Otjozondjupa, des Kambazembi-Stammes und des Hererolandes*. Windhoek. Self-published. [Consult Namibiana Buchdepot].

Ohly, R. (1990). *The Poetics of Herero Song*. Windhoek: University of Namibia.

Olusoga, D., & Erichsen, C. W. (2010). *The Kaiser's Holocaust: Germany's Forgotten Genocide and the Colonial Roots of Nazism*. London: Faber and Faber.

Pool, G. (1979). *Die Herero Opstand 1904–1907*. Cape Town: HAUM.

Report on the Natives of South West Africa and their Treatment by Germany: Presented to Both Houses of Parliament by Command of His Majesty. (1918). London: H.M.S.O.

Sarkin, J. (2011). *Germany's Genocide of the Herero: Kaiser Wilhelm II, His General, His Settlers, His Soldiers.* Cape Town: University of Cape Town Press.

Silvester, J., & Gewald, J.-B. 2(003). *Words Cannot Be Found. German Colonial Rule in Namibia: An Annotated Reprint of the Blue Book.* Leiden: Brill.

Utley, J. (2017). *The Lie of the Land.* Windhoek: University of Namibia Press.

Vedder, H. (1973). *Das Alte Südwestafrika, Südwestafrikas Geschichte bis zum Tode Maharero 1890.* Windhoek: SWA Wissenschaftliche Gesellschaft. Zweite Auflage.

Vedder, H. (1934). *Das Alte Südwest.* Berlin: Verlag Martin Warneck.

Vedder, H. (2016). *South West Africa in Early Times.* Being the story of South West Africa up to the date of Maharero's death in 1890. Namibian Scientific Society. Reprinted edition.

Wallace, M. (2011). *A History of Namibia from the Beginning to 1990.* Johannesburg: Jacana.

Zimmerer, J., & Zeller, J. (2008). *Genocide in German South-West Africa: The Colonial War (1904–1908) in Namibia and its aftermath.* Monmouth, Wales: Merlin Press.

In 2019, the United States Holocaust Memorial Museum library in Washington DC commissioned an annotated bibliography of the books they hold concerning the genocide. The bibliography, created by Dr Elizabeth R. Baer, Research Professor in English and African Studies at Gustavus Adolphus College in the US, can be consulted here: https://www.ushmm.org/collections/bibliography/herero-and-nama-genocide.

A podcast in which Dr. Baer discusses her book *The Genocidal Gaze* can be found at: https://newbooksnetwork.com/elizabeth-r-baer-the-genocidal-gaze-from-german-southwest-africa-to-the-third-reich-wayne-state-up-2017/

Who is Katjivena?

After Uazuvara Ewald Kapombo Katjivena (born February 1941) left Namibia for exile early in 1964, he held several leadership posts in SWAPO. He became Head of Programmes for SWAPO's English and Otjiherero broadcasts that were carried on Radio Tanzania and Zambia's external broadcasting services. These programmes were beamed to Namibia to counteract the South African propaganda in the country.

He became the Deputy SWAPO Representative in Cairo, Egypt, and a short while later, he was appointed SWAPO Chief Representative in Algeria. He subsequently became Deputy Secretary for Foreign Affairs, as well as a member of SWAPO's Executive Committee.

Over the years, Katjivena carried out numerous missions for SWAPO, including being part of the SWAPO delegation to the Tricontinental Conference held in Cuba in 1965.

Katjivena and I were given the task of organising the first international conference on the liberation struggle of Namibia, held in Brussels, Belgium, in 1972. In preparation for this conference, we accompanied the SWAPO President Sam Nujoma on a tour of Scandinavian countries, aimed at mobilising public opinion in support of the liberation struggle of our country. In Oslo we met with Prime Minister Trygve Bratteli, who was in fact the first Prime Minister to receive our delegation.

Katjivena is a skilful communicator and an accomplished linguist. He speaks Otjiherero, French, German, English, Dutch, Arabic and Norwegian. He is well versed in international affairs and is appreciative of the many cultures he has been exposed to during his life. As a filmmaker and a member of senior management at the Namibia Broadcasting Corporation (NBC), he made a significant contribution to NBC in the first years after independence, when it was the voice of a new Namibia and an important instrument for informing and educating the public. In his later years, from his base in Norway, he has lectured on Africa and worked with the integration of refugees.

Dr Peter H. Katjavivi
Speaker of the National Assembly of Namibia

www.ingramcontent.com/pod-product-compliance
Lightning Source LLC
Chambersburg PA
CBHW071413300426
44114CB00016B/2284